Taschentrainer

Barry Baddock / Susie vrobel

Update Your Business Vocabulary

Die wichtigsten Wörter für Büro und Business

Hueber Verlag

Taschentrainer Englisch

ist eine Reihe von Übungsbüchern im kleinen Format für schnelles und bequemes Üben zu Hause und unterwegs. Mit den Taschentrainern werden Grammatik, Wortschatz und Sprachgebrauch in authentischen Situationen wiederholt, gefestigt und vertieft. Die Reihe ist optimal für das Selbststudium geeignet.

3. 2. 1. | Die letzten Ziffern
2014 13 12 11 10 | bezeichnen Zahl und Jahr des Druckes.
Alle Drucke dieser Auflage können, da unverändert,
nebeneinander benutzt werden.
1. Auflage

Redaktion: Heike Birner, Hueber Verlag, Ismaning
Umschlaggestaltung: Parzhuber und Partner, München
Fotogestaltung Cover: wentzlaff | pfaff | güldenpfennig kommunikation Gmbh, München
Coverfoto: © Matton Images/StockByte
Zeichnungen: Irmtraud Guhe, München
Layout und Satz: Birgit Winter, Seefeld
Druck und Bindung: Ludwig Auer GmbH, Donauwörth
Printed in Germany
ISBN 978-3-19-257918-9

Inhalt

Vorwort

Liebe Englischlernende,

die *Taschentrainer Englisch* sind ideal für das schnelle und bequeme Lernen zwischendurch. Das kleine, handliche Format passt in jede Tasche. So können Sie jederzeit, zu Hause und unterwegs, Übungen machen.

Der vorliegende Taschentrainer hilft Ihnen, Ihren englischen Wortschatz für das Berufsleben systematisch zu festigen und zu erweitern. Alle wichtigen Themen werden behandelt – von der Bewerbung auf Englisch über Firmenstruktur und Büroalltag bis hin zum internationalen Handel. Einen Überblick über die Themenbereiche erhalten Sie durch das Inhaltsverzeichnis auf Seite 3.

In diesem Taschentrainer finden Sie

- über 150 abwechslungsreiche und unterhaltsame Übungen;
- authentische Situationen und Kontexte aus dem Berufsleben;
- einen übersichtlichen Lösungsteil zur Selbstkontrolle und mit ergänzenden Erklärungen.

Der vorliegende Taschentrainer ist als Begleitmaterial für die Kompetenzniveaus A2 bis B1 des Europäischen Referenzrahmens konzipiert. Er eignet sich bestens zur Evaluation, um zu testen, was man gut oder weniger gut beherrscht.

Viel Spaß mit Ihrem Taschentrainer!

Autoren und Verlag

A. Bewerben

1. Useful vocabulary
2. Getting a job
3. CV expressions
4. Building phrases
5. Building sentences
6. British vs. American English
7. Matching pairs
8. A letter of application
9. Replying to the invitation
10. Typical mistakes
11. The job interview
12. Translate
13. Odd man out
14. Forming expressions
15. Complete the application
16. Abbreviations

A1 Useful vocabulary

Ordnen Sie jedes Wort einer Liste zu.

position • experience • salary

List A	List B	List C
education	wages	post
qualifications	earnings	appointment
skills	commission	vacancy
abilities	bonus	opening
______	______	______

A2 Getting a job

Setzen Sie die Wörter in der richtigen Reihenfolge ein.

acceptance • application • interview • ~~job ad~~ • offer • shortlist

job ad ▶	▶	
▶	▶	

A3 CV expressions

Ergänzen Sie die englischen Ausdrücke und ordnen Sie sie den deutschen zu.

pr_s_ _t
em_ _ _y_r

appl_ _ _tion
f_ _m

c_v_r_ng
l_t_ _r

ed_c_tional
b_ _kgr_ _nd

m_r_t_l
st_t_s

1. heutige/r Arbeitgeber/in: ____________________
2. Bewerbungsformular: ____________________
3. Begleitschreiben: ____________________
4. Schul-/Ausbildung: ____________________
5. Familienstand: ____________________

A4 Building phrases

Verbinden Sie die Ausdrücke.

1. enrol →	a. by doing
2. lack	b. enquiries
3. learn	c. experience
4. make	d. in a course
5. enclose	e. overtime
6. take	f. copies
7. work	g. responsibility

1	2	3	4	5	6	7
d						

A5 Building sentences

Verbinden Sie die Satzteile.

I ...

1. enclose copies
2. am enrolled in
3. may lack sales
4. took responsibility
5. am highly flexible and willing to work
6. am accustomed to learning by doing

a. a Business Skills course at the local college.
b. and to working independently.
c. experience but am qualified in wholesale management.
d. for Despatch and Deliveries.
e. of my certificates and qualifications.
f. overtime, including weekends.

1	2	3	4	5	6
e					

A6 British vs. American English

Ergänzen Sie die fehlenden Buchstaben.

1.
BE: h_l_d_y
AE: v_c_tion
(Urlaub)

2.
BE: progr_m_e
AE: progr_m
(Programm)

3.
BE: t_ck
AE: ch_ck
(abhaken)

4.
BE: fill _n
AE: fill o_t
(ausfüllen)

A7 Matching pairs

Setzen Sie die Wörter im Kasten so ein, dass Wortpaare entstehen.

alphabetical • ~~business~~ • part-time • permanent
senior • specialised

1. home address — *business* address
2. temporary position — ______ position
3. junior manager — ______ manager
4. general knowledge — ______ knowledge
5. full-time work — ______ work
6. chronological order — ______ order

A8 A letter of application

Nummerieren Sie die Textteile in der richtigen Reihenfolge.

____ As requested, I enclose a CV in English and would like to point out that I am available for interview at any time.

____ I am writing about the trainee management position advertised on your website.

____ Yours sincerely,

____ I would like to apply as I would welcome the challenge and may have the qualifications you are looking for.

____ I look forward to hearing from you.

____ To the Personnel Manager
Raydon International
Dear Mr Carter,

A9 Replying to the invitation

a. Lesen Sie zunächst diese Einladung und Ihre handschriftlichen Notizen.

Reference: Your application / Trainee Manager

Dear ...

After studying your application, our committee have put your name on a shortlist of four applicants. We would be pleased if you could come for an interview, together with the other applicants.

Ich kann!

The interviews will take place here on
Monday, 11th May, commencing 2pm. *Nach 15hr?*

(muss aus Frankfurt fliegen!)

We are prepared to pay your travel expenses from Frankfurt and back.

Would you kindly email to let me know if you wish to attend the interview?

Soll ich Gutachten usw. mitbringen?

With best wishes,

Harold Carter
Committee Secretary

b. Vervollständigen Sie nun Ihr Antwortschreiben.

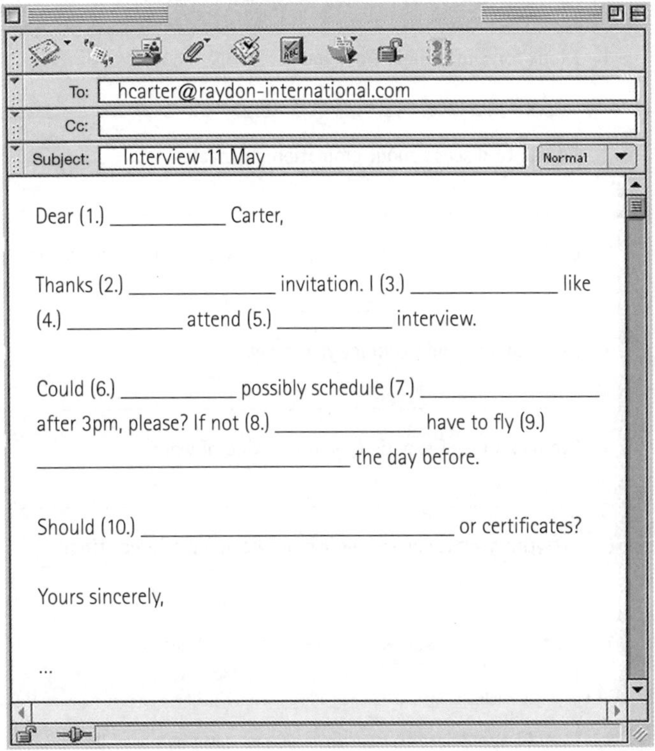

To: hcarter@raydon-international.com

Cc:

Subject: Interview 11 May

Dear (1.) ____________ Carter,

Thanks (2.) _______________ invitation. I (3.) _______________ like (4.) ____________ attend (5.) ____________ interview.

Could (6.) ____________ possibly schedule (7.) ___________________ after 3pm, please? If not (8.) _______________ have to fly (9.) _________________________________ the day before.

Should (10.) _________________________________ or certificates?

Yours sincerely,

...

A10 Typical mistakes

Korrigieren Sie diese grammatikalisch falschen Sätze.

1. I look forward to hear from you.

   I look forward to hearing from you.

2. I'd like to discuss about promotion prospects.

   ____

3. Could you say me something about the company management?

   ____

4. I told that I would contact you today.

   ____

5. I've had a lot of experiences in this kind of work.

   ____

6. Everything what you've told me has been most interesting.

   ____

7. For two years, I worked by Germelmann & Braun.

   ____

8. I would appreciate to hear from you as soon as possible.

   ____

A11 The job interview

Ordnen Sie die Gesprächsbeiträge in der richtigen Reihenfolge an.

a. And thirdly, I feel I have exactly the right qualifications for the job.

b. Would you tell us why you applied for this position?

c. But you've had no direct experience of working in this field, have you?

d. Good. We think they are too.

e. Oh, I'd welcome that. I work well under pressure.

f. That's good to hear. And your second reason?

g. That's true, but I'm very keen to learn.

h. The salary and the prospects, frankly. They're very attractive.

i. Well, three reasons basically. First, I've always wanted to work in this field.

j. You'd have to work to very tight deadlines, you know.

Correct order:

b									

A12 Translate

Übersetzen Sie ins Englische.

1. *Ich bin an der Stelle interessiert, die Sie ausgeschrieben haben.*
   (position – advertised)

   I am interested in the position you have advertised.

2. *Ich lege meinen Lebenslauf und mein Schulabgangszeugnis bei.*
   (enclose – CV – a copy – school certificate)

   ____

3. *Ich möchte einen Termin vereinbaren.*
   (arrange – appointment)

   ____

4. *Ist meine Bewerbung vertraulich?*
   (confidential)

   ____

5. *Ich stehe jederzeit für ein persönliches Gespräch zur Verfügung.*
   (available – any time)

   ____

6. *Mein letzter Arbeitgeber ist bereit, mir eine Referenz zu schreiben.*
   (willing – provide)

   ____

7. *Zu meinen Aufgaben gehörte Handelskorrespondenz.*
   (duties – correspondence)

   ____

A13 Odd man out

Streichen Sie jeweils den Ausdruck durch, der nicht passt.

1. full-time – part-time – overtime – half-time – ~~in time~~
2. form – application – reference – interview – testimonial
3. married – single – widowed – independent – divorced
4. basic – ambitious – elementary – intermediate – advanced
5. place of birth – place of residence – home page – home address – business address
6. maternity leave – annual holidays – leave of absence – time off – probation period
7. salary – contract – wage – earnings – bonus
8. co-operative – efficient – enterprising – hopeful – reliable
9. engage – appoint – resign – hire – employ
10. vacancy – opening – position – appointment – profession
11. trained – retrained – enclosed – skilled – semi-skilled

A14 Forming expressions

Verbinden Sie die Ausdrücke.

to …

1. apply for
2. submit
3. fill in
4. write somebody
5. enclose
6. create
7. arrange
8. deal with
9. work
10. be paid

a. a CV
b. a form
c. a good impression
d. a job
e. a problem
f. a reference
g. an application
h. an interview
i. by the hour
j. under pressure

1	2	3	4	5	6	7	8	9	10
d									

A15 Complete the application

Vervollständigen Sie diese E-Mail anhand der 6 Ausdrücke.

available for interview • flexible and willing • foreign clients
references and testimonials • regional sales • the opportunity

During my employment with Schmidt & Horn, I was responsible for (1.) ____________________. This involved meeting (2.) ____________________ frequently, and negotiating with them in German or English. I also had (3.) ____________________ to familiarise myself with wholesale methods.

I would like to point out that I am (4.) ____________________ to work extra hours at short notice. I am (5.) ____________________ at any time and can send copies of my (6.) ____________________ on request.

A16 Abbreviations

Schreiben Sie die Abkürzungen aus.

1. CV: Curriculum Vitae
   (Curclm Vte)

2. MBA: ______
   (Mstr of Bsns Admnstrtn)

3. d/b: ______
   (dte of bth)

4. OT: ______
   (ovtme)

5. rep: ______
   (sales rprsntatve)

6. PRP: ______
   (prfrmnce-rltd pay)

7. PA: ______
   (Prsnl Asstnt)

8. HR: ______
   (Hmn Resrces)

9. PR: ______
   (Pblc Rltns)

B. Bei der Arbeit

1. Useful vocabulary
2. In the office
3. Anagrams
4. British vs. American English
5. Making an appointment
6. Receiving a visitor
7. Arranging the parts
8. Introductions
9. Translate
10. Conference expressions
11. A speech of welcome
12. True or false?
13. Typical mistakes
14. Abbreviations

B1 Useful vocabulary

Ordnen Sie jedes Wort einer Liste zu.

equipment • scanner • repairs

List A	List B	List C
security	materials	photocopier
maintenance	stationery	shredder
running costs	supplies	calculator
rent	furniture	printer
______	______	______

B2 In the office

Ordnen Sie den Bildern die englischen Wörter zu.

ballpoint • desk • envelope • paper clip • punch • scissors

1. ______

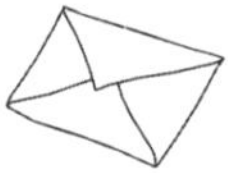

2. ______

3. ______

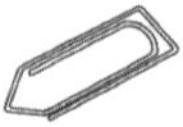

4. ______

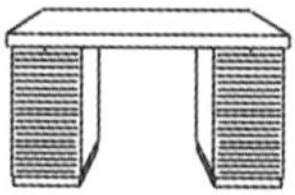

5. ______

6. ______

B3 Anagrams

Ordnen Sie die Buchstaben so an, dass die englischen Übersetzungen entstehen.

1. RATTY NOISE (= *Schreibwaren*): stationery
2. UNTRUE FIR (= *Möbel*): ____________
3. ANCIENT NAME (= *Wartung*): ____________
4. RUSTY ICE (= *Sicherheit*): ____________
5. RED HERDS (= *Aktenvernichter*): ____________
6. OUR CATCALL (= *Taschenrechner*): ____________
7. RENT RIP (= *Drucker*): ____________

B4 British vs. American English

Verbinden Sie die entsprechenden britischen, amerikanischen und deutschen Ausdrücke.

British English	American English	German
1. post room	a. eraser	6. *Radiergummi*
2. rubber	b. thumbtack	7. *Poststelle*
3. caretaker	c. ZIP code	8. *Postleitzahl*
4. drawing pin	d. mail room	9. *Reißzwecke*
5. postcode	e. janitor	10. *Hausmeister/-in*

(Example: 1. post room → d. mail room → 7. Poststelle)

1	2	3	4	5
d				
7				

B5 Making an appointment

Sie leiten eine Firma in Berlin und haben diese E-Mail erhalten. Lesen Sie die E-Mail und den Eintrag in Ihrem Terminkalender.

Subject: September meeting

Normal

Dear ...,

Just a short mail to let you know that I'll be in Berlin in September. I would welcome the opportunity to meet you again and to discuss our new catalogue with you – in particular, our new attractive models of swivel chair, workdesk and security cabinet.

It would be convenient if we could meet on the 21st, as I already have a lunch appointment in Berlin on that day.

May I ask you to suggest a meeting time? I think about an hour would do.

With best wishes,

Sarah Crawcour

Mo: 21 September

0900 – 1100	*Dortmund: Braun & Hinkel*
1145	*flight to Berlin*
1330 – 1500	*Geithner*
1600 – 1700	*Lindemann*

Vervollständigen Sie nun diese Antwort.

Dear (1.) ______________

Many thanks (2.) ______________ mail. I (3.) ______________ looking forward (4.) ______________ Berlin. I (5.) ______________ here at (6.) ______________ September. Could (7.) ______________ please confirm (8.) ______________ that time?

In the attachment (9.) ______________ directions and a map (10.) ______________ find our offices. Please (11.) ______________ me if (12.) ______________ any difficulty.

Yours (13.) ______________

...

B6 Receiving a visitor

Ordnen Sie diese Wörter richtig an.

1. be Mr must Wilson you
   You must be Mr Wilson.
2. meet nice to you
   ____
3. come could glad you
   ____
4. did a good have trip you
   ____
5. please a seat take
   ____
6. at home make yourself
   ____
7. coffee a cup like of would you
   ____

B7 Arranging the parts

Ordnen Sie die Dialogteile in der richtigen Reihenfolge an.

a. Ah, you must be Mr Broome. Nice to meet you. Glad you could come.

b. Did you have a good trip?

c. Well, please take a seat. And make yourself at home.

d. Would you like a cup of coffee before we begin?

Frau Dechert

e. I did, thank you.

f. No thank you. We can begin straight away, if you like.

g. Oh, I'm very glad to be here.

h. That's very kind of you.

Mr Broome

Correct order:

a							

B8 Introductions

Lesen Sie diese Gesprächsbeiträge beim gegenseitigen Bekanntmachen und beantworten Sie dann die folgenden Fragen.

Mr James, I'd like you to meet Herr Bremer, our accounts manager. Kai, this is Mr James from Leeds. As you know, Mr James may soon be our agent in Britain.

Yes, indeed. How do you do, Mr James. I'm glad you could come.

Nice to meet you, Herr Bremer. I'm very pleased to be here.

And may I introduce Frau Peters, who also works in our accounts section? Frau Peters, Mr James, our guest from Leeds.

How do you do, Frau Peters.

And this is Herr Weber, who's in charge of consultancy and services here. Herr Weber, I think you and Mr James met at the Trade Fair in Munich, didn't you?

Yes, we did. Nice to see you again, Mr James.

Likewise, Herr Weber. How are you?

1. How many people are in the room? ☐
2. How many work in the same section? ☐
3. How many has Mr James met before? ☐

B9 Translate

Übersetzen Sie ins Englische.

1. *Für unser nächstes Treffen schlage ich Mittwoch, den 21. vor.*
   (meeting – 21st)
   For our next meeting, I suggest Wednesday the 21st.
2. *Ich schlage vor, wir treffen uns um 10 im Foyer.*
   (lounge)
   ______
3. *Ich hole Sie um 11 Uhr im Hotel ab.*
   (pick – up – o'clock)
   ______
4. *Darf ich Sie zum Mittagessen einladen?*
   (invite – lunch)
   ______
5. *Sagen Sie mir Bescheid, falls Sie auf Schwierigkeiten stoßen.*
   (run into any difficulty)
   ______
6. *Betrachten wir einmal die Hauptaspekte, mit denen wir uns hier befassen müssen.*
   (look at – deal with)
   ______
7. *Wenn Sie bereit sind, können wir gleich anfangen.*
   (ready – straight away)
   ______
8. *Es ist sehr angenehm, mit Ihnen Geschäfte zu machen.*
   (a pleasure – do business)
   ______

B10 Conference expressions

Bilden Sie aus diesen 14 Wörtern 7 englische Ausdrücke und ordnen Sie sie den deutschen zu.

~~attendance~~ • break • card • coffee • conference • fact • keynote
~~list~~ • name • opening • session • sheet • speaker • timetable

1. *Anwesenheitsliste:* attendance list
2. *Eröffnungssitzung:* ______________________
3. *Hauptredner/-in:* ______________________
4. *Infoblatt:* ______________________
5. *Kaffeepause:* ______________________
6. *Konferenzprogramm:* ______________________
7. *Namensschild:* ______________________

B11 A speech of welcome

Stellen Sie sich vor, Sie veranstalten eine Tagung. Üben Sie anhand dieser Notizen Ihre Begrüßungsworte.

All hear me?
Introduce myself
Welcome to conference – pleasant journey?
Everything satisfactory?
Couple of points:
(a) Need a help? See me (main entrance)
(b) All have fact sheet + conference timetable + name card?
(c) Please sign attendance list
Coffee break: 11am
Lunch (restaurant): 1pm
Questions?

B12 True or false?

Lesen Sie diese E-Mail und entscheiden Sie, ob die folgenden Aussagen richtig oder falsch sind.

Subject: Conference / 2 August

Normal

Dear Frau Meyer,

I am pleased to confirm your booking for a half-day conference on Thursday, 2 August. As requested, I have reserved the Regency Room for 25 participants. It will be available to you from 12.30pm until 6.30pm. OHP and projector will be provided as part of our service.

Our business centre facilities (including internet access, photocopier and light refreshments) will be available free of charge to your conference participants.

If you prefer a particular seating arrangement, please inform me in advance.

For your convenience, our restaurant is open from 10.30am to 8.30pm. In the attachment, I enclose menu and prices. Please note that a 5% discount is available for advance bookings at the restaurant.

I look forward to seeing you in August. Thank you for booking at Branley Hall Hotel.

Yours sincerely,

Stephan Dawes
Senior Manager

	True	False
1. The conference will take place on one afternoon in one room.	☐	☐
2. The participants may use the business centre.	☐	☐
3. They have to pay for photocopies.	☐	☐
4. Frau Meyer has asked for a specific seating arrangement.	☐	☐
5. Meals at the restaurant can be booked in advance.	☐	☐

B13 Typical mistakes

Wählen Sie die korrekten Verbformen.

1. Did you remember **informing / to inform** the sales staff about the meeting?
2. I remember **discussing / to discuss** the problem with Mr Dawes when he visited us.
3. If we stop **mailing / to mail** clients, we'll have to call them instead.
4. I stopped **having / to have** lunch about 1.30.
5. Let's go on **using / to use** this data till we get an update.
6. We'll now go on **dealing / to deal** with the big issue of sales contracts.

B14 Abbreviations

Vervollständigen Sie die Tabelle mit Hilfe der unten aufgeführten Listen.

English abbreviations	English meanings	German abbreviations
1. eg (Latin: *exempli gratia*)	*for example*	*z. B.*
2. ie (Latin: *id est*)		
3. etc (Latin: *et cetera*)		
4. cf (Latin: *confer*)		
5. pp (Latin: *per procurationem*)		

English meanings	**German abbreviations**
and the rest	*d.h.*
compare	*i.A.*
for and on behalf of	*usw.*
for example	*vgl.*
that is	*z.B.*

C. Die Firma

1. Useful vocabulary
2. Describing the firm
3. Company work
4. Make verbs
5. Who's in charge?
6. Company structure
7. Find synonyms
8. Change the words
9. British vs. American English
10. Finding the expressions
11. Completing the report
12. Typical mistakes
13. Translate
14. True or False?
15. Abbreviations

C1 Useful vocabulary

Ordnen Sie jedes Wort einer Liste zu.

medium-sized • firm • section

List A	List B	List C
enterprise	department	small
company	division	large
business	unit	substantial
____________	____________	____________

C2 Describing the firm

Vervollständigen Sie diese E-Mail mit den Wörtern im Kasten.

company • department • enterprise • firm • section • substantial

Subject: Company structure

Normal

Now let me tell you something about the (1.) c____________, which is a medium-sized one – our production (2.) d____________ has only 10 staff. And there are just four full-time workers in the sales (3.) s____________. Now, that's really quite small for an (4.) e____________ like ours. But, as we want to be a leading (5.) f____________ in our industry, we've been investing a lot in research. So our research department is quite (6.) s____________ – 12 full-time staff.

C3 Company work

Was passt zusammen?

to
1. be
2. do
3. sign
4. make

a. a contract
b. a decision
c. business
d. in charge of accounts
e. responsible for sales

1	2	3	4
d,			

C4 Make verbs

Setzen Sie die entsprechenden Verben ein.

1. manufacturer: to *manufacture* garden furniture
2. division: to ____________ a section into two parts
3. sales: to ____________ at the best price
4. director: to ____________ an advertising campaign
5. executive: to ____________ a task successfully
6. management: to ____________ a sales department
7. equipment to ____________ an office
8. location to ____________ a problem
9. promotion to ____________ an employee (to a higher position)

C5 Who's in charge?

Ordnen Sie die Dialogbeiträge in der richtigen Reihenfolge an.

a. Are you the Managing Director, Mr Lyle?

b. And you have three sections under you?

c. Oh, who's responsible for Manufacturing?

d. Ah, that's run by Bob Rawlins, isn't it?

a visitor

e. It is, yes. And then there's Sally Lawson. She's in charge of Accounts.

f. That's Jill Bradley. Then there's Marketing.

g. Yes, I am.

h. Yes. First, there's Manufacturing.

Mr Lyle

Correct order:

a							

C6 Company structure

Sehen Sie sich den Dialog in C5 noch einmal an und tragen Sie die zugehörigen Abteilungen ein.

____
(Ray Lyle)

____
(Jill Bradley)

____
(Bob Rawlins)

____
(Sally Lawson)

C7 Find synonyms

Suchen Sie in diesem Ausschnitt aus einem Firmenbericht 6 Wörter mit der gleichen Bedeutung wie 1. – 6.

> We have recently made two changes to the organisation of the firm. First, our main office is now located in Eisenach. Second, our Finance Department now has two sections: Accounts and Sales. Ms Larson is in control of Accounts and Mr Dawes heads the Sales section. Mr Dawes' responsibilities include pricing and ordering.

1. company ___firm___
2. situated ______________
3. divisions ______________
4. in charge ______________
5. manages ______________
6. duties ______________

C8 Change the words

Ersetzen Sie jeweils einen Buchstaben, um die englischen Übersetzungen zu erhalten.

1. SERVILE *(= Dienstleistung)* service
2. DEAD *(= Leiter/-in)* ____________
3. BRUNCH *(= Niederlassung)* ____________
4. LOSS *(= Chef/-in)* ____________
5. RESORT *(= Bericht)* ____________
6. DECODE *(= entscheiden)* ____________
7. REMAIL *(= Einzelhandel)* ____________
8. EMPLOYER *(= Arbeitnehmer/in)* ____________

C9 British vs. American English

Verbinden Sie die entsprechenden britischen, amerikanischen und deutschen Ausdrücke.

British English	American English	German
1. estate agent	a. incorporated (Inc)	6. *stiller Teilhaber*
2. limited (Ltd)	b. silent partner	7. *Immobilienmakler*
3. noticeboard	c. sales tax	8. *schwarzes Brett*
4. sleeping partner	d. realtor	9. *Mehrwertsteuer*
5. value added tax	e. bulletin board	10. *GmbH*

1	2	3	4	5
d				
7				

C10 Finding the expressions

Verbinden Sie die Wörter in den Kästen, um die unten aufgeführten Ausdrücke zu übersetzen.

financial • industrial • joint • office • policy • progress • quality

control • director • meeting • premises • report • site • venture

1. *Leiter der Finanzabteilung:* ____________________
2. *Industriegelände:* ____________________
3. *Büroräume:* ____________________
4. *Strategiebesprechung:* ____________________
5. *Fortschrittsbericht:* ____________________
6. *Qualitätskontrolle:* ____________________
7. *Beteiligungsunternehmen:* ____________________

C11 Completing the report

Benutzen Sie nun die englischen Ausdrücke, die Sie in C10 gebildet haben, um diesen Firmenbericht zu vervollständigen.

Every Monday, the company management have a (1.) p____________, sometimes at our (2.) i____________ in Berlin, but usually at our (3.) o____________ in Potsdam. The (4.) f____________ presents a (5.) p____________ at the meeting. Then important issues are discussed, such as the question of (6.) q____________ or our (7.) j____________ with Broadways.

C12 Typical mistakes

Achten Sie beim Korrigieren dieser Sätze auf die fettgedruckten Wörter.

1. That report is no longer **actual** – here's the latest one.

   That report is no longer current – here's the latest one.

2. First, I'll give you some **informations** about the company structure.

3. Then I'll **explain you** our hiring policy.

4. **The most producers** in this field are based in Asia.

5. The management will be meeting on the first Tuesday of the month, **as usually.**

6. **The news are** good: sales increased 8% last month.

C13 Translate

Übersetzen Sie ins Englische.

1. *Wir haben jede Woche eine Strategiebesprechung.*
   (We – policy meeting – week)
   We have a policy meeting every week.

2. *Das neue Unternehmen beschäftigt 28 Mitarbeiter.*
   (The new company – workforce – 28)

3. *Wir haben in arbeitssparende Technologie investiert.*
   (We've been – labour-saving)

4. *Normalerweise führen wir Reparaturen selbst durch.*
   (We – carry out – ourselves)

5. *Für diesen Geschäftsbereich ist Herr Peterson verantwortlich.*
   (Herr – is – for – this part – operation)

6. *Die Techniker sind für die Überwachung der Sicherheit verantwortlich.*
   (The – monitoring safety)

7. *Alle Entscheidungen über die Lieferungen werden von Frau Berner getroffen.*
   (All – about deliveries – made – Berner)

8. *Wir reichen Frau Berner jeden Monat einen Fortschrittsbericht ein.*
   (We hand in – progress – month)

C14 True or False?

Lesen Sie diese Beschreibung und kreuzen Sie an, ob die folgenden Aussagen richtig oder falsch sind.

We work a flexitime system, so staff can decide on their own hours to a certain extent. But we are having some recruiting problems at the moment. Because, you know, it's difficult to find suitable trainees when you're located on a greenfield site, quite far from any major city, as we are. In many respects, it's a very good location, though. Good road system, plenty of storage and delivery space. And three of our suppliers are right here, on the same site. And, for the first five years, we're paying a low rent, thanks to the relocation scheme operated by the local council.

	True	False
1. All the staff are free to decide which hours they will work.	☐	☐
2. It's hard for the company to find suitable trainees.	☐	☐
3. The company is short of delivery space.	☐	☐
4. Three of the company's suppliers are on the greenfield site.	☐	☐
5. The relocation scheme allows the company to pay a low rent.	☐	☐

C15 Abbreviations

Schreiben Sie die Abkürzungen aus indem Sie die Wörter im Kasten kombinieren. Zwei der Wörter kommen mehr als einmal vor.

Chief • Chamber • Commerce • Company • Office • Officer
Director • Executive • Fair • Financial • Managing • Trading

1. MD *(= Vorstandsvorsitzende/r, Geschäftsführer/-in)*

   Managing Director

2. CEO *(= Chef/in eines Großkonzerns (U.S.A.))*

   ____

3. CFO *(= Leiter/in der Finanzabteilung)*

   ____

4. Co *(= Gesellschaft)*

   ____

5. C of C *(= Industrie- und Handelskammer (= IHK))*

   __________ of __________

6. OFT *(= Amt für Verbraucherschutz (UK))*

   __________ of __________

D. Handel

D1 Useful vocabulary

Ordnen Sie jedes Wort einer Liste zu.

research • shipment • invoice

List A	List B	List C
quotation	market	freight
estimate	planning	cargo
guarantee	strategy	carriage
licence	analysis	consignment
____________	____________	____________

D2 What price?

Ordnen Sie die englischen Ausdrücke den deutschen zu.

1. purchase		a. *Verkaufspreis*
2. market		b. *angemessener Preis*
3. fair		c. *Einkaufspreis*
4. unit	price	d. *fester Preis*
5. buying		e. *Kaufpreis*
6. selling		f. *Stückpreis*
7. fixed		g. *Marktpreis*

1	2	3	4	5	6	7
e						

D3 More prices

Vervollständigen Sie die Ausdrücke.

1. *günstiger Preis:*

   fvrble price

   ____

2. *Sonderpreis:*

   spl price

   ____

3. *konkurrenzfähiger Preis:*

   cmptitve price

   ____

4. *Katalogpreis:*

   lst price

   ____

5. *niedrigster Preis:*

   btm price

   ____

6. *Durchschnittspreis:*

   avge price

   ____

D4 Trading expressions

Verbinden Sie die entsprechenden englischen und deutschen Ausdrücke.

1. three-year	a. order	6. *Nachbestellung*
2. door-to-door	b. point	7. *drei-jährige Garantie*
3. break-even	c. delivery	8. *Kostendeckungspunkt*
4. first-time	d. guarantee	9. *Neukunde*
5. follow-up	e. customer	10. *Haus-zu-Haus Lieferung*

1	2	3	4	5
d				
7				

D5 Make verbs

Setzen Sie die entsprechenden Verben ein.

Verbs from nouns:

1. quotation: We ___quote___ all our prices in Euros.
2. estimate: I'll have to ____________ the transport costs.
3. planning: We ____________ to keep prices unchanged.
4. analysis: I'll ____________ the figures before I call you.

Verbs from adjectives:

5. favourable: We ___favour___ rail transport for this particular delivery.
6. special: They ____________ in high-gloss printing.
7. competitive: We don't ____________ with the big manufacturers.
8. average: We ________________ 45 orders a week.

D6 Make nouns

Tragen Sie die entsprechenden Nomen ein.

verb	noun	verb	noun
1. to assist	*assistance*	8. to ship	________
2. to guarantee	________	9. to document	________
3. to deliver	________	10. to regulate	________
4. to forward	________	11. to haul	________
5. to package	________	12. to fly	________
6. to weigh	________	13. to store	________
7. to sell	________	14. to receive	________

D7 Make adjectives

Tragen Sie die entsprechenden Adjektive ein.

1. competition: *competitive*
2. acceptance: ________
3. analysis: ________
4. guarantee: ________
5. information: ________
6. profit: ________
7. strategy: ________
8. structure: ________
9. transport: ________

D8 Talking business

Ein Exporteur spricht mit einem Kunden. Setzen Sie diese Ausdrücke an den passenden Stellen ein.

door-to-door • ~~follow-up~~ • guarantee • list price • quotation • shipment • special price

On (1.) ___follow-up___ orders over 500 units, we give a 3% discount on the (2.) ______________.

Right. Now, how soon could you send a (3.) ______________ of 600 units?

600? You'd have them in 3 days, sir. That'll be (4.) ______________ delivery.

And your two-year service (5.) ______________ is included, isn't it?

Included in our (6.) ______________. Yes, sir.

Right. I've made a note of that.

Would you like me to mail that (7.) ______________ to you, sir?

D9 Tag questions

Fügen Sie die entsprechenden Frageanhängsel ein.

couldn't you? • didn't we? • ~~aren't they?~~ • don't you?
haven't you? • isn't it? • shouldn't we?

1. They're working to a very close profit margin, *aren't they* ?
2. You know our terms of contract, ______________________?
3. We made this point clear to you, ______________________?
4. You've read the terms of delivery, ______________________?
5. You could email those figures to us, ______________________?
6. The main aim is to reduce transport costs, ______________________?
7. We should settle this as soon as possible, ______________________?

D10 Transport

Verbinden Sie die englischen Wörter zu Wortpaaren und ordnen Sie sie den deutschen Ausdrücken zu.

agent • air • airtight • by • date • delivery • forwarding
freight • ~~gross~~ • in • packaging • sea • transit • ~~weight~~

German	English
1. *Bruttogewicht*	*gross weight*
2. *Liefertermin*	______________
3. *luftdichte Verpackung*	______________
4. *Luftfracht*	______________
5. *Spediteur*	______________
6. *unterwegs*	______________
7. *auf dem Seeweg*	______________

D11 British vs. American English

Vervollständigen Sie die Wörter. Achtung: Die deutschen Übersetzungen enthalten 3 Fehler. Können Sie sie finden?

British English	American English	German
cheque	1. c_ _ _k	*Scheck*
current account	2. c_ _ _ _ing account	*Sparkonto*
3. g_ _ds train	freight train	*Eilzug*
note/banknote	4. b_ _l	*Geldschein*
5. r_ _lway	6. r_ _lroad	*Autobahn*
7. registered p_ _t	8. registered m_ _l	*Einschreiben (= versichert)*
unit trust	9. mutual f_ _d	*Investmentfonds*

D12 Change the words

Ersetzen Sie jeweils einen Buchstaben, um die englischen Übersetzungen zu erhalten.

1. TRACE (= *Handel*): trade
2. PRIMING (= *Preisfestsetzung*): ____________
3. FOE (= *Gebühr*): ____________
4. BALL (= *Rechnung*): ____________
5. CHANGE (= *berechnen*): ____________
6. EXPANSIVE (= *teuer*): ____________
7. FOODS (= *Waren*): ____________
8. SEAL (= *verkaufen*): ____________

D13 An answerphone message

Eine Kollegin hat auf Ihrem Anrufbeantworter eine Nachricht für Mr Howes hinterlassen. Übersetzen Sie die Nachricht für ihn mithilfe der englischen Ausdrücke.

> Hier ist Susanne Briegel. Ich rufe aus Essen an. Bitte sagen Sie Mr Howes, dass Leyland Shipping mich angerufen hat, und dass sie gesagt haben, sie liefern morgen Auftragsnummer 133 (Bruttogewicht: 5,2t). Es ist nicht nötig, mich zurückzurufen. Vielen Dank.

Mr Howes,

____

____

____

____

D14 Translate

Ordnen Sie die englischen Wörter so, dass eine korrekte Übersetzung entsteht.

1. *Wir werden den Versand arrangieren.*
   We the arrange will shipment

   We will arrange the shipment

2. *Wir können Ihnen eine Lieferung von Haus zu Haus anbieten.*
   We delivery can door-to-door offer you

3. *Die Lieferungen müssen zwei Monate vorverlegt werden.*
   Deliveries be brought forward have months to two by

4. *Unsere Kunden wollen den Preis des Produkts wissen.*
   Our price customers know of product the the to want

5. *Wir werden unter dem Marktpreis verkaufen, um die Lagerbestände loszuwerden.*
   We'll below get market of price rid sell stock the to

6. *Wir waren in der Lage, die voraussichtlichen Kosten abzuschätzen.*
   We've able been costs estimate likely the to

7. *Könnten Sie mir darauf eine Garantie geben?*
Could a give guarantee me on you that?

____

8. *$770 für 10 Stück – das ist ein Durchschnittspreis von $77.*
$770 that's for 10 average of units an price $77

____

9. *Wir müssen noch weitere $450 verdienen, um kostendeckend zu arbeiten.*
We'll another break make even need to to $450

____

10. *Für jede Bestellung wird eine Liefergebühr erhoben.*
There's charge a delivery each for order

____

D15 About the competition

Vervollständigen Sie diesen Geschäftsbericht mit Hilfe der Wörter.

advertising • discount • network • operate • roughly • strong

There is only one (1.) ____________ competitor in the region: Lawley & White. They have (2.) ____________ a 30% share of the market. So we have been looking at how Lawley & White (3.) ____________.

They revise their (4.) ____________ and their product catalogues every six months. And they have a (5.) ____________ of agents in the region. In addition, their prices are very competitive and they offer a 10% (6.) ____________ on first orders.

D16 Abbreviations

Schreiben Sie die Abkürzungen mit Hilfe der Vorgaben aus.

1. POS (= pt of sle): point of sale
2. USP (= uniq sllng pt): ______
3. PIN (= Prsnl Idntfctn Nmbr): ______
4. B2B (= bsnss to bsnss): ______
5. B2C (= bsnss to cstmr): ______
6. jit (= jst in tm): ______
7. FAO (= fr the attn of): ______
8. IMO (= Intntnl Mny Odr): ______
9. DIY store (= do-it-yslf store): ______
10. CAD (= cmptr-aided dsgn): ______
11. DTP (= dsktp pblshng): ______
12. IT (= inftn tchnlgy): ______

E. Geschäftsreisen

1. Useful vocabulary
2. Confirming travel arrangements
3. Hotel check-in
4. Travel expressions
5. Verb – adjective – noun
6. Negotiating: useful phrases
7. Working out a deal
8. Giving a presentation
9. British vs. American English
10. Till or by?
11. Keeping an appointment
12. Socializing
13. Translate
14. Abbreviations

E1 Useful vocabulary

Ordnen Sie jeden Ausdruck einer Liste zu.

publicity video • single room • problem areas

List A	List B	List C
key issues	reception desk	flip chart
main questions	room service	overhead projector
discussion points	wake-up call	power point
______________	______________	______________

E2 Confirming travel arrangements

Bestätigen Sie Ihre Reisedaten, indem Sie diese E-Mail mit den Ausdrücken im Kasten vervollständigen.

by 1430hr • due to • key issues • pick me up • publicity video

Dear Mr Lloyd,

Many thanks again for offering to (1.) ______________ at Stansted Airport on Tuesday the 15th. I can confirm that I am (2.) ________________ arrive at 0932hr. I have to travel on to London after our meeting. So I must be at Stansted Station (3.) ______________, in order to take the train to London Liverpool Street. This will certainly leave us enough time to see the (4.) ____________________ and to discuss (5.) ______________.

I am looking forward to seeing you.

Yours sincerely,

Barbara Horn

E3 Hotel check-in

Barbara Horn spricht in ihrem Londoner Hotel mit der Rezeption. Ordnen Sie die Gesprächsteile in der richtigen Reihenfolge an.

a. Ah, yes, that's it. Right, Ms Horn. Here's your key. Room 322. And I'll have your luggage brought up directly.

b. Mr Barnes is in the bar right now, I believe. Just through that door and turn right.

c. For two nights, you say? When did you reserve, please, Ms Horn?

d. Good morning. What can I do for you?

Hotel Receptionist

e. About two weeks ago, from my company office. Oh, maybe you have the reservation under my company's name: Berber & Horn.

f. Thank you. Just one more thing: I'm expecting to meet a Mr Barnes here.

g. Good, thank you. I'll go and find him now.

h. Good morning. My name's Horn. I have a reservation – a single room with bath, for two nights.

Barbara Horn

Correct order:

d							

E4 Travel expressions

Kombinieren Sie diese Wörter zu 9 Ausdrücken aus dem Themenbereich Reisen, die den deutschen Wörtern entsprechen.

bag • ~~business~~ • car • carry-on • check • domestic • flight
hire • intermediate • local • return • security • service
shuttle • stop • ticket • time • ~~trip~~

1. *Geschäftsreise:* business trip
2. *Sicherheitskontrolle:* ______
3. *Handgepäck:* ______
4. *Autovermietung:* ______
5. *Inlandflug:* ______
6. *Zwischenlandung:* ______
7. *Pendelverkehr:* ______
8. *Ortszeit:* ______
9. *Rückfahrkarte:* ______

E5 Verb – adjective – noun

Schreiben Sie die entsprechenden Adjektive und Nomen in die Tabelle.

verb	adjective	noun
1. negotiate *(= verhandeln)*	negotiated	negotiation
2. propose *(= vorschlagen)*		
3. agree *(= zustimmen)*		
4. approve *(= genehmigen)*		
5. solve *(= lösen)*		
6. decide *(= entscheiden)*		
7. advise *(= empfehlen)*		

E6 Negotiating: useful phrases

Verbinden Sie die 7 bei Verhandlungen benutzen Ausdrücke mit den entsprechenden Beschreibungen.

List A

1. As I was saying ...
2. We do normally insist on ...
3. Do you really think ...?
4. Could I break in here?
5. I'd like to come back to ...
6. Now, let's look at ...
7. I'm willing to meet you halfway.

List B

a. Coming to terms *(sich einigen)*
b. Emphasising *(Betonen)*
c. Interrupting *(Unterbrechen)*
d. Proposing next steps *(die nächsten Schritte vorschlagen)*
e. Questioning an opinion *(in Frage stellen)*
f. Referring back *(auf etw. zurückkommen)*
g. Resuming *(Fortfahren)*

1	2	3	4	5	6	7
g						

E7 Working out a deal

Barbara Horn verhandelt mit Mr Barnes. Vervollständigen Sie den Dialog mit diesen 5 Verben.

agree • insist • meet • order • suggest

So you're offering us an introductory discount of 5%?

5% off the catalogue price, yes – if you (1.) ____________ 500 units now. Would you like to place an order?

Well, that depends on the terms of payment, Frau Horn. I (2.) ____________ we pay 50% in advance, and the remaining 50% in six months.

We do normally (3.) ____________ on full payment on delivery, Mr Barnes.

This is a substantial order. Surely you could (4.) ____________ to a later final payment.

Look, I'm willing to (5.) ____________ you halfway, Mr Barnes. I suggest you pay 75% on delivery, and the remaining 25% in six months. That's a very good offer.

E8 Giving a presentation

Hier sehen Sie einen Teil von Barbara Horns Präsentation in London. Finden Sie die 7 englischen Ausdrücke, die den deutschen in der Liste entsprechen.

> I'd like you to look at this graph. It shows our total exports for the year. And, as you see, here on the right of the screen, it highlights the recent increase in orders. Would you like to raise any questions at this point? No? So, let's go on to the next charts, which convey an idea of the age range in the market. They also show the comparison between the spending habits of ...
>
> Oh, I'm sorry. Looks like we have a slight problem. I'm sure it's just a glitch. If you'll just wait a moment, please, I'll get this fixed ...

1. *zeigen:* show
2. *eine Idee übermitteln:* ____________
3. *Fragen stellen:* ____________
4. *Funktionsstörung:* ____________
5. *hervorheben:* ____________
6. *Leinwand:* ____________
7. *Vergleich:* ____________

E9 British vs. American English

Setzen Sie die fehlenden Ausdrücke ein.

British English	American English	German
Underground	subway	1. ____________
2. ____________	elevator	*Aufzug*
ground floor	first floor	*Erdgeschoss*
first floor	3. ____________	*erster Stock*
second floor	4. ____________	*zweiter Stock*

E10 Till or by?

Setzen Sie **by** oder **till** ein:

1. We can leave the question of transport ______________ the 20th.
2. I have to reach Stansted Station ______________ 12.15.
3. If you can't deliver ______________ the end of the week, we'll have to find another supplier.
4. They've accepted cash payments ______________ now, but soon they'll only take credit cards.

E11 Keeping an appointment

Herr Hardt wird während einer Geschäftsreise von einem Kunden begrüßt. Vervollständigen Sie den Dialog.

Herr Hardt: Good morning. (1.) ______________ name is Hardt. (2.) ______________ appointment with Mrs Lawson.
Mrs Lawson: Ah, Herr Hardt. I'm Dora Lawson. I'm pleased to meet you.
Herr Hardt: I'm pleased (3.) ______________ you too, (4.) ______________ Lawson.
Mrs Lawson: Did you have a good flight?
Herr Hardt: Oh, yes, very smooth. (5.) ______________ arrived (6.) ______________ time (7.) ______________ happy to say.
Mrs Lawson: Right, would you like to have a rest before we start?
Herr Hardt: No, (8.) ______________ ready (9.) ______________ start when you are, (10.) ______________ Lawson.
Mrs Lawson: How about a cup of tea or coffee?
Herr Hardt: Well (11.) ______________ tea (12.) ______________ very welcome.

E12 Socializing

Zwei Geschäftspartner unterhalten sich zwanglos.
Setzen Sie Frau Zuthers Gesprächsbeiträge ein.

Frau Zuther's parts:
And it's a break from the daily grind, isn't it?
Do you enjoy the travel side of your work, Mr Jackson?
Do you travel a lot?
How do you mean?
I know the feeling!
OK, we'll try and go easy on you!

Frau Zuther: (1.) ____________________

Mr Jackson: Oh, yes, very much indeed. But I've got a young family now. Anything longer than two days away from home – and I begin to have a guilty conscience!

Frau Zuther: (2.) ____________________

Mr Jackson: Oh, every three weeks or so. Of course, it's always nice to fly away and see something new.

Frau Zuther: (3.) ____________________

Mr Jackson: Well, yes and no. I mean, working in a small, competitive business means putting in a lot of hours. So it's great to get away ...

Frau Zuther: (4.) ____________________

Mr Jackson: ... but there's always work to be done once you get there – today's discussions, for example.

Frau Zuther: (5.) ____________________

Mr Jackson: I'd appreciate it! Oh, and another advantage of business trips: it's the only time I can catch up with news.

Frau Zuther: (6.) ____________________

Mr Jackson: Well, reading newspapers on the journey. And magazines. Otherwise, the only news I get is half-an-hour of TV – if I'm lucky!

E13 Translate

Übersetzen Sie ins Englische.

1. *Sie sagten, Sie werden dort sein, um mich am Flughafen zu treffen.*
   (You – there – meet me – airport)

   You said you'll be there to meet me at the airport.

2. *Wie werde ich Sie erkennen?*
   (How – recognise?)

   ____

3. *Wurde eine Nachricht für mich hinterlassen?*
   (Has there been – please?)

   ____

4. *Ich hoffe, es ist alles zu Ihrer Zufriedenheit.*

   (I – you find – your satisfaction)

   ____

5. *Sollten Sie Hilfe benötigen, lassen Sie es mich bitte wissen.*
   (Should – any – please – know)

   ____

6. *Zögern Sie nicht, jederzeit Fragen zu stellen.*
   (Don't hesitate – any time)

   ____

7. *Gibt es noch weitere Fragen?*
(Are there any –?)

____

8. *Ich würde Ihnen gerne ein kurzes Video zeigen.*
(I'd like – video)

____

9. *Könnten Sie mir sagen, was es kostet?*
(Could – price, please?)

____

10. *Würde Ihnen diese Vereinbarung passen?*
(Would – arrangement – convenient – you?)

____

11. *Auf den ersten Blick sieht die Idee gut aus.*
(On – face of it – idea – good)

____

12. *Könnten Sie das Angebot noch zwei Wochen aufrecht erhalten?*
(Could – keep – open – weeks?)

____

13. *Wir müssten auf einer Vorauszahlung bestehen.*
(We'd have – insist – advance payment)

____

E14 Abbreviations

Schreiben Sie die Abkürzungen aus. Die Wörter im Kasten helfen Ihnen dabei.

~~audio~~ • automated • cassette • compact • conference • disc
display • machine • overhead • projector • recorder • teller
unit • video • video • ~~visual~~ • visual

1. A/V ______ *audio visual* ______
2. ATM ____________________
3. CD ____________________
4. OHP ____________________
5. VC ____________________
6. VCR ____________________
7. VDU ____________________

F. Handelskorrespondenz & Telefonieren

F1 Useful vocabulary

Ordnen Sie jeden Ausdruck einer Liste zu.

order • hang up • cell phone

List A	List B	List C
confirmation	receiver	connect
enquiry	handset	call back
offer	mobile	hold the line
______________	______________	______________

F2 Transaction chain

Setzen Sie die 6 Wörter in chronologischer Reihenfolge in die Kästchen ein

confirmation • delivery • enquiry • offer • order • ~~payment~~

▶	▶	*payment*
▶	▶	

F3 What sort of offer ...?

Ordnen Sie die englischen Wörter den deutschen Ausdrücken zu.

1. best
2. binding
3. firm
4. introductory
5. special
6. written

→ offer →

a. *Festangebot*
b. *schriftliches Angebot*
c. *verbindliches Angebot*
d. *Höchstangebot*
e. *Sonderangebot*
f. *Einführungsangebot*

1	2	3	4	5	6
d					

F4 ... and what sort of order?

Ordnen Sie wieder die englischen Wörter den deutschen zu.

1. advance
2. follow-up
3. initial
4. repeat
5. standing
6. trial

→ order →

a. *Dauerauftrag*
b. *Erstauftrag*
c. *Nachbestellung*
d. *Nachbestellung*
e. *Probeauftrag*
f. *Vorausbestellung*

1	2	3	4	5	6
f					

F5 Complete the proposal

Vervollständigen Sie diesen Text anhand der Wortliste.

early • leaflet • meeting • specific • suits

Dear Mr Lyle,

Specification: Injector 30/2

As requested at your recent (1.) _______________ with Frau Bittkowski, I am sending you a (2.) _______________ containing the technical data on our Injector 30/2. In order to discuss the (3.) _______________ requirements of German users, I propose another meeting in Hamburg on 11 June. Please let me know if this date (4.) _______________ you. I look forward to your (5.) _______________ reply.

Yours sincerely,

Wolfram Benz

Technical Director

F6 Business correspondence

Diese 5 E-Mails begleiteten einen Geschäftsabschluss zwischen einem (deutschen) Käufer und einem (britischen) Verkäufer. Bringen Sie die Korrespondenz in die richtige Reihenfolge.

a

Dear Herr Reinhardt,

It is a pleasure to hear from you again.
We are happy to quote you our charge of £755.- for air freight transport of 20 dozen units of Uranus, to Hamburg. Delivery: 15 March.
Your usual mode of payment will be acceptable.
Would you like to place an order?

Yours sincerely,
Bob Jordan

b

Dear Mr Jordan,

Having seen the new model Uranus on your website, we would like to receive your offer and best price for 20 dozen units to Hamburg. Delivery before 31 March.

Looking forward to hearing from you.
P. Reinhardt

c

Dear Herr Reinhardt,

We confirm receipt of your order and look forward to executing it with care. Would you please confirm delivery?

Thank you again.
Bob Jordan

d

Dear Mr Jordan,

Thank you for your prompt reply. Please accept this as our order for the goods quoted. We look forward to taking delivery 15 March.

Regards,
P. Reinhardt

e

Dear Mr Jordan,

This is to confirm that we have taken delivery of 20 dozen units (model: Uranus) today. Thank you for the careful packaging and execution of our order.

Regards,
P. Reinhardt

Correct order:

b				

F7 Phoning about an order

Herr Reinhardt telefoniert mit einem anderen Zulieferer. Versuchen Sie, anhand der Hilfen beide Gesprächsbeiträge auf Englisch zu formulieren.

1. *Hier ist Peter Reinhardt. Ich rufe aus Hamburg an und möchte gern mit Ms Johnson sprechen.*
   This – Reinhardt – calling – like to speak – please.

   ____

   ____

2. *Es tut mir leid, sie telefoniert gerade, Herr Reinhardt. Vielleicht kann ich Ihnen helfen?*
   I'm afraid – the other line at the moment – help you?

   ____

   ____

3. *Ja, würden Sie Ms Johnson bitte ausrichten, dass wir das 'de Luxe'-Modell bestellen werden?*
   Yes, please tell – order – model.

   ____

   ____

4. *Das 'de Luxe'-Modell.*
The – model.

____

____

5. *Aber nur, wenn Sie diesen Monat liefern können. Würden Sie das noch einmal für mich wiederholen?*
But only – deliver – month – run that back to me, please?

____

____

6. *In Ordnung: Sie werden das 'de Luxe'-Modell bestellen, wenn wir diesen Monat liefern können.*
OK – order – this month.

____

____

7. *In Ordnung.*
Right.

8. *Gut, Herr Reinhardt, ich richte es aus. Sie hören sehr bald wieder von Ms Johnson. Vielen Dank für Ihren Anruf.*
Very well – pass that on – be hearing – very soon – for calling.

____

____

F8 Telephone phrases

Ordnen Sie die Ausdrücke der Liste B den Beschreibungen der Liste A zu.

List A

1. Getting through
2. Asking for someone to call back
3. Asking the speaker to make something clear
4. Saying you'll call back later
5. Checking you've understood the speaker
6. Making sure the speaker has understood you
7. Ending the call

List B

a. Could you get back to me on that later, please?
b. Do call me again if I can be of any help.
c. I'll phone you again as soon as possible.
d. Let me read that back to make sure I've got all of it.
e. Would you give me that information once more, please?
f. Would you put me through to Mr Handley, please?
g. Would you run that back to me, please?

1	2	3	4	5	6	7
f						

F9 Typical mistakes

Achten Sie beim Korrigieren dieser Sätze auf die fettgedruckten Wörter.

1. We'll need a few days to make **an analyse** of your offer.

   We'll need a few days to make an analysis of your offer.

2. We would **appreciate to receive** your reply soon.

3. **Despite of** the damage, the goods are still useable.

4. The orders section has **an own website**.

5. **In the moment**, Frau Bach isn't in. Can she call you back?

6. Could you use different packaging, **without that you charge** extra?

F10 Spell your name!

Können Sie Ihren Namen am Telefon buchstabieren? Versuchen Sie es!

The International Telephone Alphabet

A for Andrew	J for Jack	S for Sugar
B for Benjamin	K for King	T for Tommy
C for Charlie	L for Lucy	U for Uncle
D for David	M for Mary	V for Victory
E for Edward	N for Nellie	W for William
F for Frederick	O for Oliver	X for X-Ray
G for George	P for Peter	Y for Yellow
H for Harry	Q for Queenie	Z for Zebra
I for Isaac	R for Robert	

Example:

My name is Ruddock. That's R for Robert, U for Uncle, Double-D for David, O for Oliver, C for Charlie, K for King. That's Ruddock.

F11 True or False?

Lesen Sie diese Anfrage und bewerten Sie die Aussagen unten als wahr oder falsch.

For the attention of Mr Doug Saunders
Managing Director
W. Hardy & Co
...

Dear Mr Saunders,

We have seen from your website that you produce furniture designed for office use. We serve customers who may be interested not only in your furniture but also in your office accessories, including picture frames and lamps.

Unfortunately, your website lacks technical descriptions of your products. So that we can meet our customers' requirements in every respect, we would like you to send us such descriptions.

Please let us know, too, if you would be prepared to design furniture to meet individual customers' needs. We would also like to know if you offer discounts for large orders.

If your products and terms of sale are satisfactory, we will be happy to place a trial order with you.

We hope to hear from you soon.

Yours faithfully,
W. Lutz

Sales Director
Lutz & Lutz GmbH

Lutz & Lutz GmbH ...	True	False
1. sell furniture.	☐	☐
2. also produce office accessories.	☐	☐
3. have visited the other company's website.	☐	☐
4. have read the technical descriptions.	☐	☐
5. are placing a trial order for furniture and office accessories.	☐	☐
6. design furniture for individual customers.	☐	☐
7. want to know about discounts.	☐	☐

F12 British vs. American English

Bilden Sie Wortpaare, indem Sie die entsprechenden Wörter einsetzen.

1. BE: neighbour / AE: ____________________
2. BE: ____________________ / AE: theater
3. BE: modelled / AE: ____________________
4. BE: ____________________ / AE: defense
5. BE: dialogue / AE: ____________________
6. BE: ____________________ / AE: anesthetic

F13 Translate

Übersetzen Sie mithilfe der vorgegebenen Wörter ins Englische.

1. *Wenn wir diese Waren bis Ende nächster Woche nicht erhalten haben …*
   If by don't end get goods of the the those we week ...

   If we don't get those goods by the end of the week ...

2. *… muss ich den Auftrag stornieren.*
   ... I'll cancel have order the to

3. *Rufen Sie wegen der Kataloge an?*
   Are about calling catalogues the you?

4. *Könnte ich mit dem Verantwortlichen für den Verkauf sprechen?*
   May for I person responsible sales speak the to?

5. *Könnte ich mit jemandem über Ihre Liefergebühren sprechen?*
   Could about charges delivery I someone speak to your?

6. *Würden Sie mich bitte zurückrufen, um es zu bestätigen?*
   Call back confirm me please that to would you?

   ____

   ____

7. *Ich rufe Sie so bald wie möglich wieder an.*
   I'll again as as phone possible soon you

   ____

   ____

8. *Würden Sie das bitte noch einmal durchgehen?*
   Would again please run that through you?

   ____

   ____

9. *Die Ländervorwahl für Deutschland ist 49.*
   The code country Germany for is 49

   ____

   ____

10. *Rufen Sie mich bitte wieder an, falls ich Ihnen irgendwie behilflich sein kann.*
    Do again any be call can help I if me of

    ____

    ____

F14 Abbreviations

Diese Abkürzungen werden häufig in E-Mails verwendet. Schreiben Sie sie aus.

1. AFAIK
   as fr as I kw: *as far as I know*
2. ATB
   all the bst: __________
3. ATTN
   Attntn __________
4. BTW
   by the wy: __________
5. FYI
   fr yr inftn: __________
6. HTH
   hpe ths hlps: __________
7. IMO
   in my opnn: __________
8. IOW
   in othr wds: __________
9. TTYL
   tk to yu ltr: __________

G. Kommunikative Strategien

1. Useful vocabulary
2. Verbs & nouns
3. Complaining about the delivery
4. Dealing with the complaint
5. Anagrams
6. Late payment
7. Answerphone messages
8. Making things clear
9. Discussion strategies
10. Tact & discretion
11. Agreeing & disagreeing
12. Translate
13. True or False?
14. Abbreviations

G1 Useful vocabulary

Ordnen Sie jedes Wort einer Liste zu.

error • loss • repair

List A	List B	List C
adjustment	delay	blame
compensation	damage	fault
replacement	harm	mistake
______________	______________	______________

G2 Verbs & nouns

Setzen Sie die Verben und Nomen ein.

adjective	verb	noun
1. destroyed *(= vernichtet)*	destroy	destruction
2. reimbursed *(= erstattet)*	______________	______________
3. disappointed *(= enttäuscht)*	______________	______________
4. delayed *(= verspätet)*	______________	______________
5. damaged *(= beschädigt)*	______________	______________
6. disappeared *(= verschwunden)*	______________	______________
7. annoyed *(= verärgert)*	______________	______________

G3 Complaining about the delivery

Finden Sie in diesem Beschwerdeschreiben Ausdrücke, die den deutschen entsprechen.

To: h.ludwig@...

Subject: Urgent! Order F222 / Missing components

Normal

Dear Frau Ludwig,

We received your consignment yesterday, but it contains only 10 units of Type 66, not 20 units, as we ordered. This has created considerable difficulties for us, as we planned to install the units at our office immediately.

Would you please look into this matter? Most important, would you confirm that the missing 10 units will be delivered urgently? In the circumstances, we also expect compensation for this delay to our plans.

I look forward to hearing from you.

Yours sincerely,
J.H. Carter
Head Buyer

1. *Lieferung:* consignment
2. *erhebliche Schwierigkeiten:* ______
3. *sofort:* ______
4. *dringend:* ______
5. *unter den Umständen:* ______
6. *Entschädigung:* ______
7. *Verzögerung:* ______

G4 Dealing with the complaint

Hier finden Sie das Antwortschreiben auf die Beschwerde in G3. Bringen Sie die Textabschnitte in die richtige Reihenfolge.

a

Herr Kraft, our Managing Director, will be contacting you directly to discuss this with you.

b

Subject: Re: Urgent! Order F222 / Your email

CC: d.kraft@...

Dear Mr Carter,

c

I confirm that the missing 10 units are being despatched urgently. You will receive them on Tuesday. We are, of course, willing to compensate you for the difficulties you have suffered.

d

Yours sincerely,

Helga Ludwig

Sales Manager

e

In the meantime, our apologies again. I am taking firm steps to prevent such a mistake re-occurring. I trust that we can look forward to receiving further orders from you in the future.

f

I was very concerned to receive your email and have looked into the matter immediately. Unfortunately, we made the serious error of confusing your order with another customer's. On behalf of the company, I must express our sincere regret.

Correct order:

b					

G5 Anagrams

Bilden Sie Wörter aus den Anagrammen, die den deutschen entsprechen.

1. CLEAN TEMPER *(= Ersatz)*: *replacement*
2. DISCO NUT *(= Rabatt)*: ______
3. SKI TEAM *(= Fehler)*: ______
4. EAR RIP *(= Ausbesserung)*: ______
5. NO ALPINE TAX *(= Erklärung)*: ______
6. INTO SOUL *(= Lösung)*: ______
7. DUST PIE *(= Streitfall)*: ______

G6 Late payment

Ordnen Sie die Satzteile einander zu, so dass eine Beschwerde über eine überfällige Zahlung entsteht.

List A

1. We refer to our claim
2. We would like to draw your attention to the fact that
3. Furthermore,
4. Would you please
5. We trust that
6. For your convenience,

List B

a. we can look forward to receiving full payment very soon.
b. we have received no explanation for the delay.
c. for the sum of $488.60.
d. look into the matter immediately?
e. we enclose a copy of our claim.
f. payment is now four weeks overdue.
Yours faithfully,

1	2	3	4	5	6
c					

G7 Answerphone messages

Diese drei Nachrichten wurden auf dem Anrufbeantworter einer Firma hinterlassen – allesamt Beschwerden über nicht gelieferte Waren. In allen Mitteilungen fehlt der letzte Satz. Ordnen Sie die jeweils letzten Sätze den Sprechern zu.

Daniels: L&M Plating here. My name's Daniels. Look, I've been waiting all day for an order I was supposed to receive yesterday! Order 553. You assured me they'd be delivered yesterday. They still haven't arrived – and I've got a customer waiting! Look, if I don't get those goods by tonight, I'm going to cancel the order and look for another supplier.

Baldry: Hello, James & Baldry here. Sylvia Baldry speaking. I'm sorry to tell you our order hasn't arrived yet. That's Order number 554. As we were expecting to receive the goods yesterday, I was wondering what the difficulty is. You did say they'd arrive yesterday. I'm hoping you can deliver the goods today – or tomorrow at the very latest.

Rutter: Bridge Town House here. This is Brian Rutter. I'm calling to tell you that those goods we ordered – they still haven't arrived. That's Order number 555. I must say I'm disappointed. I mean, you did promise delivery by yesterday. Now, if you can get them to me right away, I'm prepared to overlook this delay. Otherwise, I'll have to consider cancelling.

Last sentences:

1: So, could you look into that for me, please?
2: So you'd better tell me what you intend to do about it!
3: So I suggest you look into the matter and let me know what's happened.

Baldry: _____ Daniels: _____ Rutter: _____

G8 Making things clear

Ordnen Sie die englischen und deutschen Ausdrücke einander zu.

1. I'll be happy to repeat that.
2. Was there something you didn't understand?
3. Would you explain that, please?
4. Can you put it differently?
5. I don't quite follow you.
6. Did I understand you correctly?

a. *Habe ich Sie richtig verstanden?*
b. *Haben Sie etwas nicht verstanden?*
c. *Ich kann Ihnen nicht ganz folgen.*
d. *Ich wiederhole das gern.*
e. *Könnten Sie das mit anderen Worten ausdrücken?*
f. *Würden Sie das bitte erklären?*

1	2	3	4	5	6
d					

G9 Discussion strategies

Ordnen Sie die gesprochenen Ausdrücke paarweise in 6 Kategorien an.

1. Inviting an opinion:
   (= eine Meinung erfragen): c + e
2. Politely disagreeing:
   (= höflich widersprechen): ___ + ___
3. Interrupting:
   (= unterbrechen): ___ + ___
4. Refusing an interruption:
   (= sich nicht unterbrechen lassen): ___ + ___
5. Considering your reply:
   (= die eigene Antwort überdenken): ___ + ___
6. Moving on to a new point:
   (= zu einem anderen Thema übergehen): ___ + ___

a. Could I come in here?
b. Could we move on now to ...?
c. How do you feel about this?
d. I can't go all the way with you on that.
e. I was wondering what you think about it.
f. I wonder if that's true.
g. Just let me complete my point.
h. Let me finish, please.
i. Let me see.
j. Let me think for a moment.
k. Perhaps I could pick up on that point.
l. There's another point we ought to discuss.

G10 Tact & discretion

Ordnen Sie die Gedanken den (taktvoll) ausgedrückten gesprochenen Sätzen zu.

Thinks ...

1. *I don't know what he means.*
2. *I don't understand this.*
3. *I don't want to do that.*
4. *I don't want to discuss that.*
5. *I've never heard anything so stupid!*
6. *I can't listen to this – I have to break in here!*

Says ...

a. *I can't quite make this out.*
b. *I can't say I'm attracted to the idea.*
c. *I'm not sure if I follow you.*
d. *Perhaps we could pick up another point here?*
e. *Excuse me – may I comment on that?*
f. *I'm afraid you've been misinformed.*

1	2	3	4	5	6
c					

G11 Agreeing & disagreeing

Ordnen Sie die Aussagen der Skala von 1 bis 5 zu.

agree 100% ◄──────────► disagree 100%

☐	☐	☐	☐	☐
1	2	3	4	5

a. I'm not sure if you're right about that.

b. I totally disagree with you.

c. I feel you're right to a certain extent.

d. I agree with you completely.

e. I'm not convinced about that at all.

G12 Translate

Übersetzen Sie ins Englische.

1. *Das war offensichtlich das Resultat Ihres Irrtums.*
   (This – clearly – error)
   This was clearly the result of your error.
2. *Die Vertragsbedingungen sind völlig klar.*
   (terms – contract – quite)
   ____
3. *Wir möchten unser tiefes Bedauern ausdrücken.*
   (wish – great regret)
   ____
4. *Bitte nehmen Sie unsere Entschuldigung entgegen.*
   (accept – apologies)
   ____
5. *Vielleicht könnte ich an diesem Punkt weitermachen.*
   (Perhaps – pick up on)
   ____
6. *Darf ich hier eine Frage stellen?*
   (May – here?)
   ____
7. *Darf ich hier einmal einhaken?*
   (Could – just come in)
   ____
8. *Lassen Sie mich bitte diesen Punkt zu Ende führen.*
   (Let – complete my point)
   ____

G13 True or False?

Lesen Sie diesen Dialog und entscheiden Sie, ob die Aussagen wahr oder falsch sind.

<u>Lars:</u> Let's see. We meet again in two weeks, right?
<u>Karin:</u> Not exactly. This time we'll meet on April the 5th.
<u>Lars:</u> Ah, yes. At 2.30.
<u>Karin:</u> Yes, not 3.30 this time. Is that still OK?
<u>Lars:</u> Oh, sure.
<u>Karin:</u> And we're meeting in another room, remember. Room 21 in the Tower Building.
<u>Lars:</u> Right you are. See you on April the 5th then. Room 21, Tower Building.
<u>Karin:</u> Oh, before you go, could we just check on who brings what?
<u>Lars:</u> Well, I'll bring the accounts.
<u>Karin:</u> Right, and I'll bring the sales projections.
<u>Lars:</u> And the estimates.
<u>Karin:</u> And the estimates, that's right. And George Land's bringing the new contract proposals.
<u>Lars:</u> Right. Are we expecting anyone else?
<u>Karin:</u> Yes, according to George's last mail, someone from the Finance Department will be coming.

	True	False
1. Lars and Karin will meet at 3.30 on 05 April.	☐	☐
2. They won't meet in the same room as today.	☐	☐
3. Lars will bring the accounts and the estimates.	☐	☐
4. Four people will be at the meeting.	☐	☐
5. A member of the Finance Department will be there.	☐	☐

G14 Abbreviations

Schreiben Sie diese Abkürzungen aus. Sie kommen oft in informeller Kommunikation per E-Mail oder SMS vor.

1. 2B: to be
2. 2day: today
3. 2morrow: ____________
4. 4: ____________
5. accomm: ____________
6. addl: ____________
7. asap: as ________ possible
8. B: ____________
9. B4: ____________
10. C: ____________
11. cd / cld: ____________
12. cttee: ____________
13. CU: ____________ you
14. esp: ____________
15. F2F: face ____________
16. incl: ____________
17. info: ____________
18. msg: ____________
19. OIC: ____________ see
20. pls: ____________
21. poss: ____________
22. R: ____________
23. recd: ____________
24. Rgds: ____________
25. spkr: ____________
26. thx / tks: ____________
27. U: ____________
28. wd / wld: ____________
29. yr: ____________
30. Yrs: ____________

H. Marketing & Werbung

H1 Useful vocabulary

Ordnen Sie jedes Wort einer Liste zu.

client • budget • slogan

List A	List B	List C
turnover	customer	logo
expenditure	consumer	image
costs	buyer	brand
______	______	______

H2 Building phrases

Verbinden Sie die entsprechenden Ausdrücke.

1. advertising	a. budget	11. *Absatzprognose*
2. annual	b. logo	12. *Adressenliste*
3. customer	c. card	13. *Werbekampagne*
4. market	d. forecast	14. *Firmenlogo*
5. promotion	e. group	15. *Jahresumsatz*
6. target	f. campaign	16. *Kundentreue*
7. company	g. loyalty	17. *Visitenkarte*
8. mailing	h. share	18. *Werbeetat*
9. business	i. turnover	19. *Zielgruppe*
10. sales	j. list	20. *Marktanteil*

1	2	3	4	5	6	7	8	9	10
f									
13									

H3 Market research

Eine Firma wendet sich an ein Marktforschungsinstitut.
Welche der 5 Sätze stammen aus dem Brief der Firma? Welche 5 Sätze stehen im Marktforschungsbericht?

1. Crossfields' prices are very competitive and they offer a 5% discount on first-time orders.
2. No steps should be taken without analysing Crossfields' methods.
3. The Eastern Region market for such services has been expanding over the last two years.
4. We think the Eastern Region may be worth exploring, to see if we ought to get into that market.
5. We want to know the size of that market and the likely demand for our services there.
6. Will people actually want such services?
7. Who are the main competitors?
8. With a 20% share of the Eastern Region market, Crossfields are the main rivals.
9. With good marketing and publicity, you could become well established in the Eastern Region.
10. What about future demand?

company's letter					
market research report	1				

H4 Finding synonyms

Ein Vertriebsagent in Irland spricht mit einem deutschen Produzenten. Finden Sie beim Lesen Ausdrücke, die denen in der Liste entsprechen.

Right, we've had a chance to examine your product closely. We've studied the specifications. And our research shows that the product has good prospects on the Irish market.

Oh, yes? You think it would sell well there?

Yes. None of your rivals have produced anything as user-friendly as this. There's just one big question.

The price?

Right. Can you make the catalogue price competitive for your particular target group?

1. investigate: *examine*
2. chances of success: ____________
3. detailed information about a product: ____________
4. competitors: ____________
5. easy to operate: ____________
6. brochure: ____________

H5 True or false?

Nach Einführung des Produkts auf dem irischen Markt schrieb der Vertriebsagent diesen Bericht. Entscheiden Sie, ob die folgenden Aussagen richtig oder falsch sind.

Subject: Interim report (Irish market)   Normal

The product is selling well on the Irish market. With its 'user-friendly' label, it has filled a niche. Market share is now 9% and we think that, realistically, you could aim for 15%.
The price is right. But it's clear that sales are not being driven by price alone. They are heavily geared to advertising. So you need to decide how much you can spend on your advertising strategy in the coming months.
Our research also suggests that you should buy more exposure on the websites of businesses in Ireland. So far, 17 traders have your name and logo on their websites. We have not yet been able to assess how much this has affected your sales. But this form of internet advertising is a more economical strategy than direct mailing or local newspaper advertising.

According to the report ...	True	False
1. The product could achieve a 15% share of the Irish market.	☐	☐
2. Advertising is influencing sales.	☐	☐
3. The producers are not spending enough on advertising.	☐	☐
4. The product is being advertised on 17 websites in Ireland.	☐	☐
5. Website advertising has not affected sales.	☐	☐
6. Direct mailing and local newspaper advertising cost more than advertising on business websites.	☐	☐

H6 Typical mistakes

Dieser Marktforschungsbericht eines deutschen Verfassers weist 6 typische Rechtschreibfehler auf. Streichen Sie die verbleibenden 5 aus und schreibe Sie die korrekten Versionen in die Liste.

> The recession has caused many customers to review their spending ~~programms~~ and to reduce their stocks. This developement has led to a sharp fall in orders for all of our products in all catagories.
>
> As a result, there is a good arguement for cutting production, but so far we have not done this. There are already signs that consumer demand will improve, but our market research commitee will be reporting on this seperately.

programmes (or: programs)	

H7 Marketing expressions

Kombinieren Sie die englischen Wörter zu 8 Ausdrücken aus dem Themenbereich Vertrieb.

behaviour • consumer • consumption • domestic • earner
group • habits • income • ~~marketing~~ • opinion • public
random • sample • sole • spending • ~~strategy~~

1. *Vertriebsstrategie:* marketing strategy
2. *öffentliche Meinung:* ____________
3. *Stichprobe:* ____________
4. *Einkommensgruppe:* ____________
5. *Alleinverdiener/-in:* ____________
6. *Verbraucherverhalten:* ____________
7. *Kaufgewohnheiten:* ____________
8. *Inlandsverbrauch:* ____________

H8 Publicity terms

Jeder dieser Ausdrücke enthält einen Buchstaben zu viel. Korrigieren Sie!

1. tirade journal *(= Fachzeitschrift)*: trade journal
2. world-of-mouth advertising *(= Mund-zu-Mund-Propaganda)*: ____________
3. scales campaign *(= Verkaufssonderaktion)*: ____________
4. purchasing powder *(= Kaufkraft)*: ____________
5. trade flair *(= Handelsmesse)*: ____________
6. business cared *(= Visitenkarte)*: ____________
7. polster *(= Plakat)*: ____________
8. prince list *(= Preisliste)*: ____________
9. freedback *(= Rückmeldung)*: ____________

H9 Translate

Übersetzen Sie ins Englische.

1. *Wir haben potenzielle Märkte in Spanien untersucht.*
   (We – investigated – Spain)
   We have investigated potential markets in Spain.

2. *Der Markt in Dänemark ist offenbar größer als erwartet.*
   (The Danish – apparently – expected)

3. *Wir haben einen gut 15%igen Anteil am Markt.*
   (We – share of –)

4. *40% der Bevölkerung gehören der mittleren Einkommensgruppe an.*
   (40% – are in – middle-income –)

5. *Wir wollen auf jeden Fall die Größe des Marktes kennen lernen.*
   (We definitely – know – size of –)

6. *Hatten Sie schon Rückmeldungen auf die Anzeige?*
   (Have – feedback – yet?)

7. *Wir haben es mit einem völlig neuen Gebiet zu tun.*
(We're dealing – entirely – territory)

____

____

8. *Das ist der Hauptvorteil dieses speziellen Modells.*
(That's – main advantage – particular –)

____

____

9. *Die Werbung nimmt 15% unseres Gesamtetats ein.*
(Advertising takes up – budget)

____

____

10. *An welche Zielgruppe richten Sie sich?*
(What – group – aiming at?)

____

____

11. *Dieses Produkt verkauft sich von selbst.*
(This – will – itself)

____

____

12. *Könnten Sie das Konzept erläutern, das hinter der Kampagne steht?*
(Could – explain the thinking behind –?)

____

____

H10 Advertising a new company

Eine deutsche Firma hat eine Niederlassung in Großbritannien eingerichtet. Diese E-Mail wurde zu Werbezwecken an Lokalblätter geschickt. Vervollständigen Sie die E-Mail mithilfe des deutschen Textes.

Dear Editor,

We / company / your area / begin production / July. We feel sure / interested / development. Please feel free / publish all or part / attached information / pictures.
You / details / website:
www.okpick.com
If / arrange / interview / photo-session, we / you. In / meantime / sending / attachments / text / photos which / hope / use / report.

Yours faithfully,

Sehr geehrter Herausgeber,

wir sind eine neue Firma in Ihrer Region und beginnen am 12. Juli mit der Produktion. Wir sind zuversichtlich, dass Ihre Leser an dieser Entwicklung interessiert sind. Sie dürfen gern den Text und die Fotos in der Anlage in vollständiger Form oder teilweise veröffentlichen. Einzelheiten finden Sie auf unserer Website:
www.okpick.com
Falls Sie ein Interview und/oder einen Fototermin vereinbaren möchten, würden wir uns sehr freuen, von Ihnen zu hören. Einstweilen schicke ich Ihnen in den Anlagen einen kurzen Text über unsere Firma sowie Fotos, die Sie hoffentlich in Ihrem Bericht verwenden können.

Mit freundlichen Grüßen

H11 Giving out a brochure

Ordnen Sie die Gesprächsbeiträge in der richtigen Reihenfolge an.

a. *So, this is our brochure. It shows you our full range.*

b. *And let me just show you page 17.*

c. *Fine. Well, do give me a call or mail me if you have any queries.*

d. *Yes, it's the first in the 'Retro' series which we're bringing out over the next six months. I think you'll like them.*

e. *Ah, yes. This is the 'Nostalgia' design you've been telling me about.*

f. *I certainly will. Thanks again.*

g. *Thank you.*

h. *Yes, well, we'll certainly be interested in looking at them.*

1	2	3	4	5	6	7	8
a							

H12 Abbreviations

Schreiben Sie die Abkürzungen aus.

1.	loc cur	*(= Landeswährung)*:	lo*cal*___ cur*rency*___
2.	HQ	*(= Hauptgeschäftsstelle)*:	he______________s
3.	CBA	*(= Kosten-Nutzen-Analyse)*:	co______ -be______ an______
4.	GNP	*(= Bruttosozialprodukt)*:	Gr______ Na______ Pr______
5.	GDP	*(= Bruttoinlandsprodukt)*:	Gr______ Do______ Pr______
6.	pa	*(= pro Jahr)*:	p______ a______
7.	i/c	*(= zuständig)*:	i______ ch______
8.	Corp	*(= Gesellschaft)*:	C______tion

H13 A SWOT analysis

Eine SWOT-Analyse berichtet über die Aussichten einer Firma.
Wofür steht SWOT? Versuchen Sie, die Wörter zu vervollständigen.

S _ _ _ _ _ _ _ _ s	*(= Stärken)*
W _ _ _ _ _ _ _ _ _ s	*(= Schwächen)*
O _ _ _ _ _ _ _ _ _ _ _ s	*(= Möglichkeiten)*
T _ _ _ _ _ s	*(= Gefährdungen)*

I. Internationaler Handel

1. Useful vocabulary
2. Import / export documents
3. The European Union
4. Joint ventures
5. Nouns & verbs
6. Discussing possibilities
7. Anagrams
8. Typical mistakes
9. Global concerns
10. World trade
11. British vs. American English
12. More documents
13. Translate
14. Abbreviations
15. Incoterms

I1 Useful vocabulary

Ordnen Sie jeden Ausdruck einer Liste zu.

economic growth • European Union • insurance certificate

List A	List B	List C
member state single market common currency	freight invoice export licence packing list	strong demand general trend business cycle
__________	__________	__________

I2 Import / export documents

Verbinden Sie die entsprechenden Ausdrücke.

1. air
2. bill of
3. insurance
4. freight
5. packing
6. export
7. despatch

a. certificate
b. invoice
c. note
d. licence
e. list
f. lading
g. waybill

8. *Ausfuhrlizenz*
9. *Frachtrechnung*
10. *Luftfrachtbrief*
11. *Konnossement*
12. *Packliste*
13. *Versandschein*
14. *Versicherungszertifikat*

1	2	3	4	5	6	7
	f					
	11					

I3 The European Union

Können Sie die Liste vervollständigen?

Member State *(= Mitgliedsstaat)*	Nationality *(= Staatsangehörigkeit)*
Austria	Austrian
Belgium	Belgian
Bulgaria	1. B____________?
Cyprus	Cypriot
2. C____________?	Czech
3. D____________?	Danish
4. E____________?	Estonian
Finland	5. F____________?
France	French
Germany	6. G____________?
7. G____________?	Greek
Hungary	Hungarian
(the Republic of) Ireland	8. I____________?
9. I____________?	Italian
10. L____________?	Latvian
Lithuania	Lithuanian
Luxembourg	Luxembourg
Malta	11. M____________?
(the) Netherlands	12. D____________?
Poland	13. P____________?
14. P____________?	Portuguese
15. R____________?	Romanian
(the) Slovakian Republic	16. S____________?
Slovenia	Slovenian
17. S____________?	Spanish
Sweden	Swedish
(the) United Kingdom	18. B____________?

I4 Joint ventures

Ein ausländischer Manager erklärt einem deutschen Geschäftsführer das Konzept eines Beteiligungsunternehmens. Sie werden beim Lesen bemerken, dass Teile seines Vortrags in der falschen Reihenfolge angeordnet sind

A. Finden Sie Ausdrücke im Text, die den deutschen entsprechen.

1. *Beteiligungs-/Gemeinschaftsunternehmen:* joint venture
2. *verhandeln:* ______
3. *Fachwissen:* ______
4. *Geräte:* ______
5. *schriftliche Absichtserklärung:* ______
6. *Verluste:* ______
7. *besitzen:* ______

A joint venture is a common way for a German company to enter the market in this country. It's a partnership in which the two companies both invest part of the capital. ...

a. The companies have to negotiate all these questions before the joint venture can really start.
b. The investments can be in the form of cash, know-how, buildings, equipment, materials or technical skills.
c. The two companies have to agree on the investments they'll make, how they'll co-operate, share profits, share risks and losses, how they'll manage the venture and who will own what.
d. Then the companies can issue a Letter of Intent.
e. This letter states that the companies are interested in starting a joint venture together. It's the basis for further discussions.

B. Ordnen Sie a. – e. in der richtigen Reihenfolge an.

b				

15 Nouns & verbs

Ordnen Sie Nomen und Verben einander zu.

Nouns

1. declaration *(= Erklärung)*: ______________________________
2. consideration *(= Erwägung)*: ______________________________
3. formation *(= Formierung)*: ______________________________
4. co-operation *(= Zusammenarbeit)*: ______________________________
5. attachment *(= Anlage)*: ______________________________
6. acceptance *(= Hinnahme, Akzeptanz)*: ______________________________
7. continuation *(= Weiterführung)*: ______________________________
8. agreement *(= Zustimmung)*: ______________________________
9. approval *(= Einverständnis)*: ______________________________

Verbs

accept attach declare
continue approve
agree form
consider co-operate

I6 Discussing possibilities

Lesen Sie diesen Dialog zwischen einer britischen Exporteurin und ihrem deutschen Kunden. Geben Sie dann an, wie sicher oder wahrscheinlich die untenstehenden Sätze sind.

So you like the look of our product, Herr Grimm. Would you like to place an order? As you know, we offer a 5% discount on the first order.

Well, I'll certainly speak to my people in Hamburg about that offer, Ms Harrington. We'll probably order five units at first ...

Excellent.

... and we may well order five more later.

Now, Herr Grimm, there's a strong possibility that the product will sell well on the German market.

That's right.

So why not order 10 units now – and get the discount on all of them?

Oh, there's little chance we can order 10 units now, Ms Harrington. Unless you offered us a bigger discount – say, 10%.

Ah, I'm sorry. My management is bound to say no to a 10% discount.

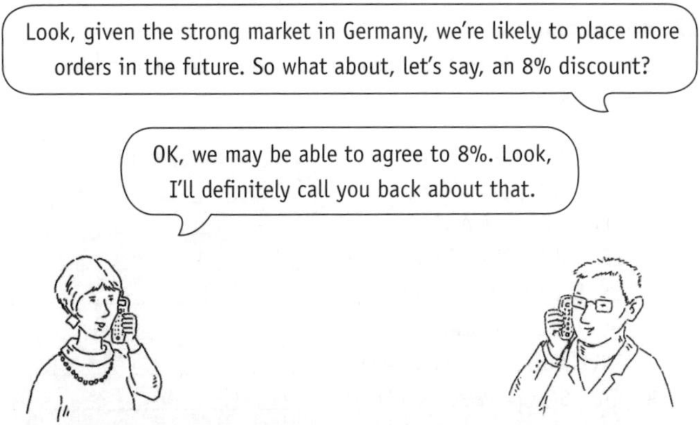

only possible *(= nur möglich)*	improbable *(= unwahrscheinlich)*
probable *(= wahrscheinlich)*	certain *(= sicher)*

1. Herr Grimm will speak to his people in Hamburg about the offer. *certain*
2. They will order five units at first. ____________
3. They will order five more later. ____________
4. The product will sell well on the German market. ____________
5. Herr Grimm's company will order 10 units now. ____________
6. Ms Harrington's management will say no to a 10% discount. ____________
7. Herr Grimm's company will place more orders in the future. ____________
8. Ms Harrington's company will agree to an 8% discount. ____________
9. Ms Harrington will call Herr Grimm back. ____________

I7 Anagrams

Ordnen Sie die Buchstaben neu an, so dass die englischen Übersetzungen entstehen.

1. ONTO A PUPIL *(Bevölkerung)*: population
2. THE AWL *(= Reichtum)*: ______
3. VERY TOP *(= Armut)*: ______
4. LEND VET POEM *(Entwicklung)*: ______
5. USABLE SATIN *(= nachhaltig)*: ______
6. GO BALL *(= weltweit)*: ______
7. INVENTOR MEN *(= Umwelt)*: ______
8. GATE SAW *(= Verschwendung)*: ______

I8 Typical mistakes

Beachten Sie beim Korrigieren dieser Sätze die fettgedruckten Ausdrücke.

1. **The modern society** depends a lot on emailing.
   Modern society depends a lot on emailing.
2. We are now discovering **that what** is meant by globalisation.
   ______
3. The representatives have no **knowledges** of German.
   ______
4. **Your both orders** have been despatched by air freight.
   ______
5. Welcome **in** Germany!
   ______
6. Our first priority is **to spare money**, then we'll think about importing
   ______

I9 Global concerns

Fügen Sie die englischen Wörter paarweise zusammen, so dass sie den deutschen Bedeutungen entsprechen.

aid • carbon • development • dioxide • disposal • economic effect • energy • food • fossil • fuels • GM • greenhouse growth • hole • line • living • noise • ozone • policy pollution • poverty • standard • ~~trade~~ • waste • ~~world~~

1. *Welthandel:* world trade
2. *Lebensstandard:* ______
3. *Armutsgrenze:* ______
4. *Wirtschaftswachstum:* ______
5. *Entwicklungshilfe:* ______
6. *Energiepolitik:* ______
7. *Treibhauseffekt:* ______
8. *Ozonloch:* ______
9. *Lärmbelastung:* ______
10. *Abfallentsorgung:* ______
11. *genmanipulierte Lebensmittel:* ______
12. *fossile Brennstoffe:* ______
13. *Kohlendioxid:* ______

I10 World trade

Bringen Sie die 10 Teile der englischen Übersetzung in die richtige Reihenfolge.

Einige Teilnehmer am globalen Markt profitieren deutlich mehr als andere. Zwar sind immer mehr Länder in den Welthandel einbezogen worden, aber gut drei Viertel des Handels finden unter den Industrieländern statt. Dagegen vereinen die 48 ärmsten Länder der Welt – in denen ein Zehntel der Weltbevölkerung lebt – gerade ein halbes Prozent des Welthandels.

Translation parts

a. Admittedly, more and more countries
b. but a good three-quarters of that trade
c. By contrast
d. clearly profit more than others.
e. comprise just a half of one percent of world trade.
f. have been drawn into world trade
g. in which a tenth of the world's population live
h. Some players on the global market
i. takes place among the industrial countries.
k. the 48 poorest countries

Correct order:

h									

I11 British vs. American English

Können Sie die 6 fehlenden Wörter einsetzen?

fall • general • inventory • mail • newsagent • petrol

British English	American English	German
inland post	domestic (1.) ______	*Inlandspost*
(2.) ______	newsdealer	*Zeitungshändler*
(3.) ______	gas / gasoline	*Benzin*
poste restante	(4.) ______ delivery	*postlagernd*
autumn	(5.) ______	*Herbst*
(6.) ______	stock-taking	*Inventar*

I12 More documents

Fügen Sie die englischen Wörter paarweise zusammen und ordnen Sie sie den deutschen Ausdrücken zu.

order • certificate • customs • delivery • health • import
insurance • invoice • permit • policy

1. *Zollfaktura:* ______
2. *Versicherungspolice:* ______
3. *Gesundheitszertifikat:* ______
4. *Importgenehmigung:* ______
5. *Lieferauftrag:* ______

I13 Translate

1. *Ungefähr 55% unserer Exporte gehen in europäische Märkte.*
   (Around – go to)
   Around 55% of our exports go to European markets.

2. *Wir erwarten nicht, dass sich der Markt vor Dezember wieder erholt.*
   (We don't – will pick up)

3. *Der Rückgang fiel in diesem Jahr stärker aus.*
   (The decline – sharper)

4. *Wie können wir entscheiden, welche Zeugnisse benötigt werden?*
   (How – certificates – needed?)

5. *Die Exporte fielen um € 1000 auf € 12000.*
   (Exports – by –)

6. *Jetzt wird der Markt gerade schwächer.*
   (Right now – weakening)

7. *Im welcher Währung müssten wir zahlen?*
   (Which currency – have to – in?)

I14 Abbreviations

Schreiben Sie die Abkürzungen aus. Einige der Wörter finden Sie im Kasten.

Administrative • Central • Chamber • Commerce • Document
Eastern • Exchange • Fund • Monetary • Single • Stock • Trade

1. WET *(= westeuropäische Zeit)*:
   Western European Time
2. CET *(= mitteleuropäische Zeit)*:
   ____
3. EET *(= osteuropäische Zeit)*:
   ____
4. IMF *(= Internationaler Währungsfonds (IWF))*:
   ____
5. WTO *(= Welthandelsorganisation)*:
   ____
6. NYSE *(= New Yorker Wertpapierbörse)*:
   ____
7. ECB *(= Europäische Zentralbank (EZB))*:
   ____
8. ICC *(= Internationale Handelskammer)*:
   ____
9. SAD Einheitspapier *(= einheitliches EU-Begleitpapier)*:
   ____

I15 Incoterms

Incoterms (**In**ternational **Co**mmercial **Terms**) sind die weltweit benutzten internationalen Handelsbedingungen. Setzen Sie die fehlenden englischen Incoterms, deren Abkürzungen oder die deutschen Übersetzungen aus dem Kasten in die Tabelle ein.

Cost And **F**reight • *Fracht, Porto bezahlt bis* • CIF • *frei längsseits Schiff* • **C**arriage **I**nsurance **P**aid • **D**elivered **E**x **Q**uay • *frei verzollt* DDU • *frei Grenze* • FCA • DES • *ab Werk* • **F**ree **O**n **B**oard

EXW	**EX W**orks	
	Free **c**arrier	*frei Frachtführer*
FAS	**F**ree **A**longside **S**hip	
FOB		*frei an Bord*
CFR		*Kosten und Fracht (nur für Schiffs-transporte)*
	Cost **I**nsurance **F**reight	*Kosten, Versicherung und Fracht bis zum Bestimmungshafen/Bestimmungsort*
CPT	**C**arriage **P**aid **T**o	
CIP		*Fracht, Porto und Versicherung bezahlt bis*
DAF	**D**elivered **A**t **F**rontier	
	Delivered **E**x **S**hip	*frei ab Schiff*
DEQ		*frei ab Kai*
	Delivery **D**uty **U**npaid	*frei unverzollt*
DDP	**D**elivery **D**uty **P**aid	

J. Mengangaben

J1 Useful vocabulary

Ordnen Sie jedes Wort einer Liste zu.

deduct • fraction • measured

List A	List B	List C
total	subtract	calculated
equation	multiply	adjusted
quantity	add	estimated
percentage	divide	converted
______________	______________	______________

J2 Anagrams

Setzen Sie mit Hilfe der Anagramme die fehlenden Wörter ein.

1. To ___*measure*___ the effect of the recession, we analyse the figures month-on-month.
   EASE RUM *(= messen)*
2. Under-18s form a big ______________ of our customers.
   CARPET GENE *(= Prozentsatz)*
3. I have to ______________ the sales commissions every week.
   ACUTE CALL *(= berechnen)*
4. We must ______________ the figures to pounds sterling.
   CORN VET *(= umrechnen)*
5. Christmas sales were only a ______________ below last year's figures.
   FAR TONIC *(= Bruchteil)*
6. We have to ______________ the cost of rent and overheads.
   BAT CRUST *(= subtrahieren)*

J3 Weekdays and months

A. Schreiben Sie die Wochentage …

1. *Sonntag:* Sunday
2. *Montag:* M______
3. *Dienstag:* T______
4. *Mittwoch:* W______
5. *Donnerstag:* T______
6. *Freitag:* F______
7. *Samstag:* S______

B. ... und die Monatsnamen auf Englisch.

1. *Januar:* ______
2. *Februar:* ______
3. *März:* ______
4. *April:* ______
5. *Mai:* ______
6. *Juni:* ______
7. *Juli:* ______
8. *August:* ______
9. *September:* ______
10. *Oktober:* ______
11. *November:* ______
12. *Dezember:* ______

J4 'Pay' or 'pay for'?

Ordnen Sie zu.

We pay …

1						

We pay for …

1. a bill
2. a car
3. a charge
4. a debt
5. a delivery
6. a meal
7. a price
8. a product
9. a service
10. a taxi
11. money
12. rent
13. somebody for doing something
14. something we have received

J5 Which date?

Diese Zeitangaben stammen vom **15. Mai**. Auf welche Daten beziehen sie sich?

1. the day before yesterday: 13th
2. three days ago: ______
3. a fortnight ago: ______
4. the day after tomorrow: ______
5. tomorrow week: ______
6. next Friday week: ______
7. a week on Friday: ______
8. in three days: ______
9. in a fortnight: ______
10. in two weeks: ______
11. in the morning: ______
12. at the end of the week: ______

MAY

M	T	W	T	F	S	S
	1	2	3	4	5	6
7	8	9	10	11	12	13
14	15	16	17	18	19	20
21	22	23	24	25	26	27
28	29	30	31			

J6 Calculating

A. Schreiben Sie die Lösungen in die Kästchen.

12 ...

added to / plus / and **3** = ☐

less / minus **3** = ☐

divided by **3** = ☐

multiplied by / times **3** = ☐

B. Ordnen Sie nun die Elemente der Listen einander zu.

List A

1. €60 + €4 → b
2. 568 x 4
3. $64 ÷ 4
4. 95.5 – 4
5. 50pcs @ $4

List B

a. 'Multiply it all by four'
b. 'Add the totals together'
c. 'Subtract four to get the final total'
d. 'Now divide by four'
e. 'Take four dollars apiece'

1	2	3	4	5
b				

J7 Discussing the numbers

Bringen Sie die Gesprächsbeiträge in die richtige Reihenfolge.

a. So if you place the order right away, we can give you a 10% discount. You'd save about £60.

b. By the 28th. Well, that would mean a special delivery. For special deliveries, we do charge a special rate.

c. We charge 10 pounds per ton or part-ton for special deliveries.

d. Give or take a few pounds, the bottom line's going to be between £530 and £550.

Supplier

e. OK, so purchase price, plus special delivery, minus the discount. What does that add up to?

f. 10% – OK, but could you deliver by the 28th? We'll be needing those new components very soon.

g. So not more than £550.

h. So how much?

Buyer

Correct order:

a		b		c		d	

J8 British vs. American English

A. Sehen Sie sich die folgenden Unterschiede bei der Angabe von Uhrzeit und Datum an.

Time:

	British + American English	**mainly British English**	**mainly American English**
08.45	eight forty-five	a quarter to nine	a quarter of nine
11.14	eleven fourteen	fourteen minutes past eleven	fourteen minutes after eleven

Date:

	British English	**American English**
12/07/10	12 July 2010 (= day/month/year)	07 December 2010 (month/day/year)
04/11/11	the 4th of November 2011	the 11th of April 2011

B. Setzen Sie nun die fehlenden Wörter in die beiden Voice-Mitteilungen ein.

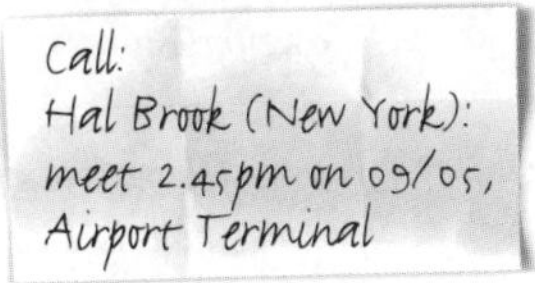

Hal, we'll be meeting at a quarter (1.) ______________ at Airport Terminal 2 on the (2.) ________________, OK?

Shirley, just to remind you: we meet at a quarter (3.) ______________ at InterCity Hotel on the (4.) ____________________________, OK?

C. Tragen Sie die Daten in der jeweils richtigen Form ein.

	British English	American English
the twenty-second of May	*22/05*	
the first of October		
the tenth of January		
the eighth of September		

J9 Expressions of quantity

Setzen Sie die fehlenden Wörter ein.

1. *every* ________ four months:	*alle vier Monate*
2. the ________ day:	*der 50ste Tag*
3. 60p ________ pound:	*60 Pence das Pfund*
4. half ________ pound:	*ein halbes Pfund*
5. half ________ hour:	*eine halbe Stunde*
6. three quarters ________ hour:	*eine Dreiviertelstunde*
7. ________ biggest:	*zweitgrößte*
8. ________ best:	*drittbeste*
9. double-________ inflation:	*zweistellige Inflationsrate*
10. a ________ of 1 to 25:	*im Verhältnis 1 zu 25*
11. ________ / ________ numbers:	*gerade / ungerade Zahlen*
12. in ________ order:	*nach Nummern geordnet*
13. three times ________ month:	*dreimal im Monat*
14. ________ the amount:	*die doppelte Summe*
15. ________ to 30%:	*bis zu 30%*

J10 Mistakes to avoid

Streichen Sie die falschen Antworten.

1. 10 kilos @ $4per kilo =
   ten kilos ...

at four dollars per kilo	~~for four dollars total~~	~~40 kilos for 40 dollars~~

2. *um halb neun* =

at half past nine	at half past eight	at half past ten

3. We're open 24/7 =

on the 24th of July	at all times	24 hours on Saturdays

4. $10.000 =

ten thousand dollars	ten thousand of dollars	ten thousands of dollars

5. 5,5% x £2.000
   The correct English form is ...

5.5% x £2,000	5,5% x £2,000	5.5% x £2.000

6. 1 customer in 3 =

the third customer	two customers	every third customer

7. *dreimal so viele* =

three times as many	three times so many	three times so much

8. *doppelt so viel* =

twice as much	double as much	double so many

J11 Exchange rates

Lesen Sie das Telefongespräch und schreiben Sie die Dollarwerte in Zahlen.

OK, you've called up the exchange rates, have you?

Yes, they're right here on the screen.

OK, first, what's the euro-to-dollar rate?

Let's see, the euro's trading at one dollar forty cents today.

One forty. Hmm, no change there. So what about pounds to dollars?

Right, one pound sterling is buying one dollar fifty-nine cents.

OK, now we've just had an order from Denmark.
So you'd better tell me the rate for the kroner.

Danish kroner? Ah, yes, here it is. Kroner to U.S. dollars.
OK, the kroner buys exactly nineteen cents today.

1. €1 = U.S. $ ________
2. £1 = U.S. $ ________
3. DKK1 = U.S. $ ________

J12 Translate

Übersetzen Sie ins Englische.

1. *Sie brauchen die Gebühren nur einmal im Monat zu bezahlen.*
   (You – charges – month)
   You have to pay charges just once a month.
2. *Jeden Monat erhalten Sie einen Auszug.*
   (Each – statement)
3. *Diese Gebühren werden von Zeit zu Zeit angepasst.*
   (These – adjusted – time)
4. *Wir werden Sie im Voraus darüber informieren.*
   (We – about – advance)
5. *Entstehen außer den Zinsen noch andere Kosten?*
   (Are there any – other than – ?)
6. *Normalerweise zahlen sie innerhalb von 30 Tagen.*
   (They – within – days)
7. *Sie verdienen ungefähr 5% mehr als im Landesdurchschnitt.*
   (They earn – above – national –)

J13 All in figures

Schreiben Sie diese Wertangaben in Zahlenform.

1. fifty times ten euros fifty: 50 x €10.50
2. six per cent of eighteen hundred pounds sterling: ______________
3. fourteen point three per cent of three and a half thousand euros:

   ____
4. two hundred and fifty at six euros twenty (each): ______________
5. two thirds of three hundred dollars: ______________
6. half a per cent: ______________

J14 Abbreviations

Schreiben Sie die Abkürzungen aus.

1. ATA: actl tme of arrvl

   actual time of arrival
2. ETA: estmtd tme of arrvl

   ____
3. am (= Latin: *ante meridiem*): btwn 12 mdnght & 12 nn

   ____
4. pm (= Latin: *post meridiem*): btwn 12 nn & 12 mdnght

   ____

K. Diagramme & Statistik

1. Useful vocabulary
2. Pie chart
3. Sales figures
4. Line chart
5. Bar chart
6. Abbreviations
7. Anagrams
8. Graphics in videoconferencing
9. Nouns & verbs
10. Translate
11. True or False?

K1 Useful vocabulary

Ordnen Sie die Diagramme ihren Bezeichnungen und Beschreibungen zu.

1. **organisation chart:** to show a hierarchy (e.g. structure of a company)
2. **bar chart:** to compare values over a period (e.g. travel costs & heating costs)
3. **line chart:** to show continuous change over a period (e.g. company sales)
4. **pie chart:** to show proportions of a whole (e.g. spending on transport: air, rail, road, sea)
5. **flowchart:** to show a continuous flow (e.g. step-by-step instructions)

a.

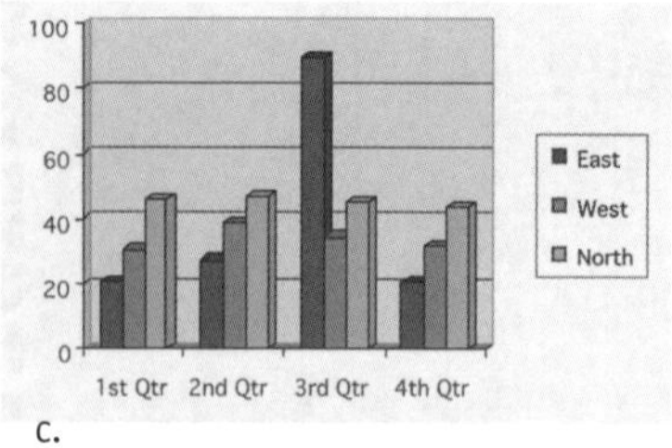

b.

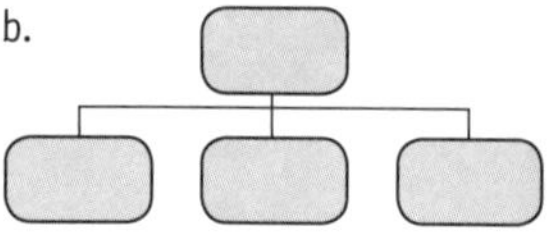

c.

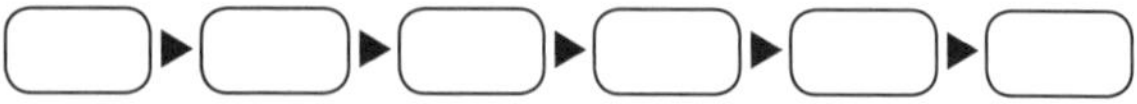

d.

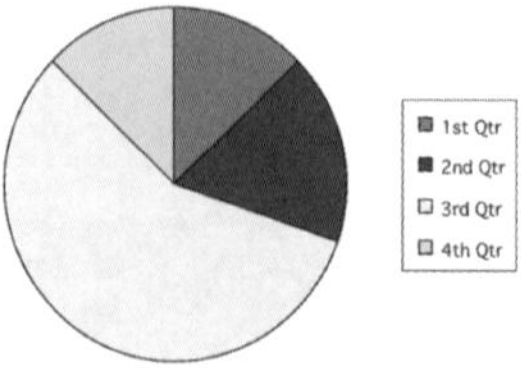

e.

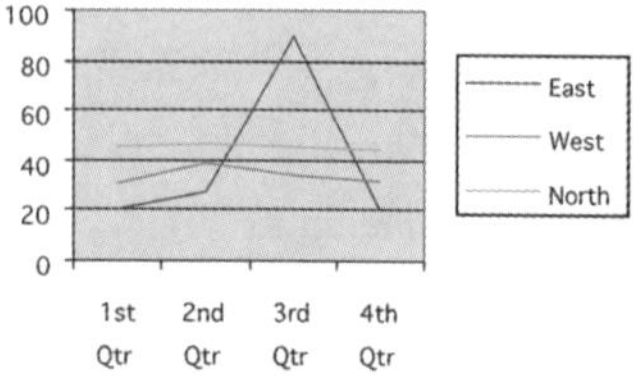

1	2	3	4	5
b				

K2 Pie chart

Büren Fitness GmbH produziert Fitnessgeräte. Dieses Kreisdiagramm zeigt die Profitverteilungen. Entscheiden Sie, ob diese Aussagen wahr oder falsch sind.

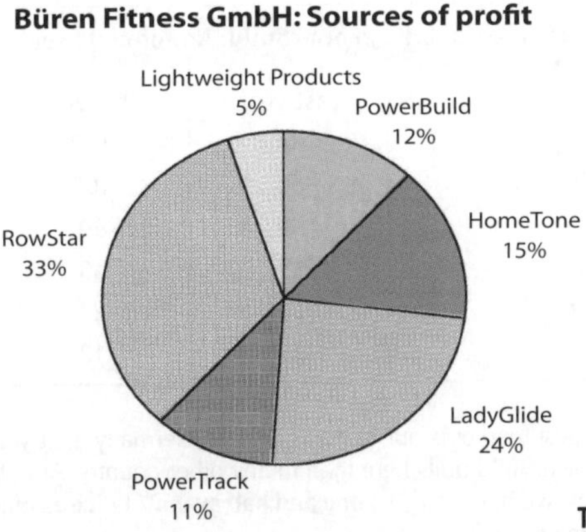

	True	False
1. Our most profitable product is RowStar.	☐	☐
2. Every third euro we get comes from selling RowStar.	☐	☐
3. LadyGlide is our fourth-biggest seller.	☐	☐
4. 15% of our profit comes from HomeTone.	☐	☐
5. Apart from our lightweight products, PowerBuild is our least profitable product.	☐	☐
6. LadyGlide brings in more profit than PowerBuild and PowerTrack combined.	☐	☐
7. We make twice as much profit from LadyGlide as from PowerBuild.	☐	☐
8. PowerTrack and PowerBuild produce almost the same amount of profit.	☐	☐
9. Lightweight products bring in the least profit.	☐	☐

K3 Sales figures

Sehen Sie sich die folgenden Absatzzahlen an. Streichen Sie dann in dem Bericht unten, der sich auf diese Zahlen bezieht, die falschen Ausdrücke.

Büren Fitness GmbH	**PowerBuild:** No. of units sold	
	Last year	This year
Germany	100	150
Scandinavia	50	100
UK	30	90
France	15	45
Austria	22	27
Spain	20	12

Our biggest market is our home market in Germany. Last year, we sold more PowerBuild units here than in any other country. And, this year in Germany, we have sold (1.) ~~**one and half again.**~~ / ~~**twice as many again.**~~ / **half as many again.**

Scandinavia is our second-biggest market for PowerBuild. Since last year, sales there (2.) **have increased twice. / have doubled. / are going the same.**

There has also been a strong increase in our UK sales. They (3.) **have increased by three / have tripled / are three times more** since last year.

PowerBuild sales elsewhere are disappointing. Compared with last year, (4.) **three times as many units / double the units / three more many units** have been sold in France. But our French market remains small. It is, in fact, the (5.) **third-least / third-smallest / smallest by a third** of our markets.

In Austria, we have seen (6.) **few increase / little increase / no increase** in PowerBuild sales. The fewest units are sold in Spain. We sell (7.) **an average of one a month / in average once a month / an average in one a month** there. In view of the poor sales in Austria and Spain, we may withdraw from those markets.

K4 Line chart

Bringen Sie die Teile des Berichts in die richtige Reihenfolge.

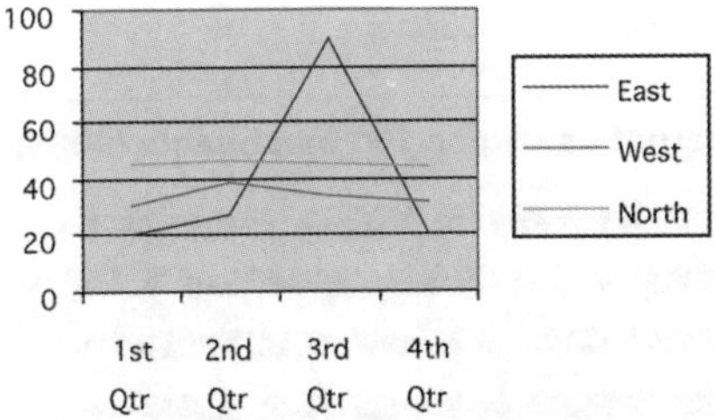

1. They reached their peak in the middle of the 3rd quarter.
2. After that, they fell sharply.
3. Sales in the East climbed only gradually at first.
4. Finally, they declined to their 1st quarter level.
5. Then there was a marked increase.

Correct order:

3				

K5 Bar chart

Im folgenden Diagramm erfahren Sie die Anzahl der Internetnutzer pro 100 Einwohner in einigen europäischen Ländern 2008. Vergleichen Sie die Daten und vervollständigen Sie die Sätze.

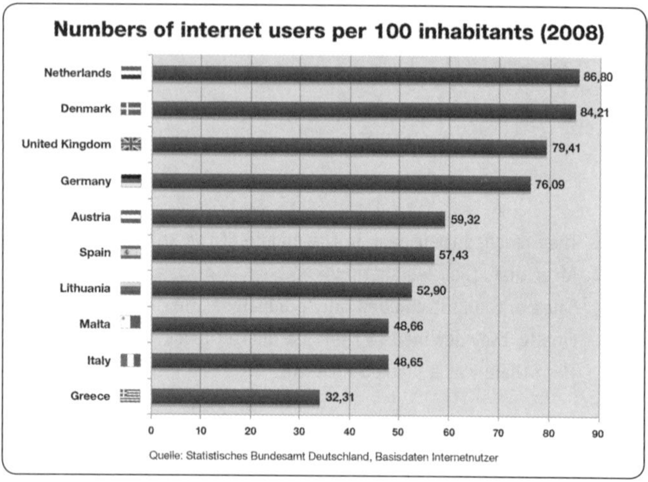

Which countries?

1. Of the 10 countries, *the Netherlands* have the highest number of internet users per 100 inhabitants.
2. __________________ has almost twice as many users per 100 inhabitants as __________________.
3. __________________ has more users per 100 inhabitants than __________________ or Malta and __________________ combined.
4. __________________ has almost as many users per 100 inhabitants as __________________.
5. In third place, the United Kingdom has about 3 per cent more users per 100 inhabitants than __________________.

How many?

Of the 10 countries ...

6. ______________ have between 80 and 90 users per 100 inhabitants.
7. ______________ have fewer than 50 users per 100 inhabitants.
8. ______________ have at least 70 users per 100 inhabitants.

K6 Abbreviations

Diese 6 Abkürzungen sind Wortpaare, die jeweils aus 2 Nomen und einem "&" bestehen. Können Sie sie ausschreiben?

English	Deutsch
1. *P&R:* ______________	*parken & pendeln*
2. *R&D:* ______________	*Forschung & Entwicklung*
3. *B&B:* ______________	*Übernachtung mit Frühstück*
4. *P&P:* ______________	*Porto & Verpackung*
5. *F&T:* ______________	*Feuer & Diebstahl*
6. *P&L:* ______________	*Gewinn & Verlust*

K7 Anagrams

Ordnen Sie die Buchstaben neu an, so dass die englischen Übersetzungen der deutschen Ausdrücke entstehen.

1. PREACH IT *(Kreisdiagramm)*: ______________
2. MANUAL EVE *(Mittelwert)*: ______________
3. VAIN AT RIO *(Variation)*: ______________
4. BIRD INTO SUIT *(Verteilung)*: ______________
5. FLAW TORCH *(Flussdiagramm)*: ______________
6. CORPS PEST *(Aussichten)*: ______________
7. ALLAY NUN *(jährlich)*: ______________

K8 Graphics in videoconferencing

Ms Layne wird von einem Techniker zu Videokonferenzen beraten. Entscheiden Sie, ob die untenstehenden Aussagen wahr oder falsch sind.

Technician: So this is your first videoconference, Ms Layne?

Ms Layne: Yes, and, to be honest, I'm hoping you can give me a few pointers on how to proceed.

Technician: Right. You'll be using some graphics, won't you? Now, my advice there is: check them all, and make sure you haven't packed too much text into them. The most important thing is that the text is readable. Because too much text on the screen makes life quite hard for the viewer.

Ms Layne: Oh, I'm sure you're right. But how much is too much? I mean, I do have to insert *some* information with my diagrams and charts.

Technician: I suggest a maximum of eight lines of text per graphic. More than that is too much.

Ms Layne: I see.

Technician: And don't try to impress your viewers with colourful graphics produced with glamorous software. It's better to aim for quality data in a clear format.

Ms Layne: Right.

Technician: And another thing: make sure you're suitably dressed. I mean: don't wear clothes with large areas of black or red or white.

Ms Layne: Why not?

Technician: Well, these colours actually prevent viewers giving you their full attention, you know?

Ms Layne: I see. So, what colours should I wear?

Technician: Oh – light blue, light green, pink. You now – light colours. And one more thing, Ms Layne: make sure you've got all your notes in order before you appear on screen. Because if you're unprepared – well, it's far more obvious onscreen than if you're face-to-face with someone!

Ms Layne: Oh, I'll be prepared – believe me, I've been preparing all week!

According to the technician ...	**True**	**False**
1. when preparing graphics, the most important point is to make the text readable.	☐	☐
2. a graphic with more than eight lines of text will create difficulties for the viewer.	☐	☐
3. lines of text should not appear with diagrams and charts.	☐	☐
4. it's more important for graphics to be in a clear format than to be colourful.	☐	☐
5. large areas of colour will create difficulties for the viewer.	☐	☐
6. prepared notes are more important in face-to-face conversation than in videoconferencing.	☐	☐

K9 Nouns & verbs

Schreiben Sie die entsprechenden Nomen zu den Verben.

1. to develop *(= entwickeln)*: ___development___
2. to highlight *(= hervorheben)*: ______________
3. to fluctuate *(= schwanken)*: ______________
4. to outline *(= Überblick geben)*: ______________
5. to flow *(= fließen)*: ______________
6. to increase *(= zunehmen)*: ______________
7. to decline *(= fallen)*: ______________
8. to expect *(= erwarten)*: ______________
9. to peak *(= einen Höhepunkt erreichen)*: ______________

K10 Translate

Übersetzen Sie anhand der Hilfen diese Diskussion über ein Absatzdiagramm.

1. *Was halten Sie von dieser Absatzkurve?*
What / think / sales curve?

2. *Nun, wir erwarten einen Rückgang am Ende des Sommers, nicht wahr?*
Well / fall-off / summer / don't we?

3. *Aber dies hier ist beunruhigend. Sehen Sie – der Rückgang ist viel stärker als zur gleichen Zeit im letzten Jahr.*
But / worrying / decline / stronger / this time / year.

4. *Die allgemeine Rezession setzt dem Handel natürlich immer noch zu. Daher wird der Absatz wahrscheinlich bis November niedrig bleiben.*
The general recession / hurting the trade / probably / flat / November.

5. *Dann erholt er sich wahrscheinlich über die Weihnachtszeit?*
Then / likely / pick up / period?

6. *Ja.*
Yes.

7. *Und wieder im Frühjahr?*
And / spring?

8. *Ja. Die Aussichten für das nächste Jahr sind tatsächlich recht gut. Haben Sie sich schon mal die Vorbestellungen angesehen, die wir erhalten haben?*
Yes. Actually, prospects / pretty good / looked at / advance orders / received?

1. *What do you think of this sales curve?*
2. ______
3. ______
4. ______
5. ______
6. ______
7. ______
8. ______

K11 True or False?

Lesen Sie diesen Text über Flussdiagramme und entscheiden Sie dann, ob die folgenden Aussagen wahr oder falsch sind.

Flowcharts are diagrams which show how steps in a process fit together. The three main types of symbol which are used in flowcharts are long circles, rectangles and diamonds. Into each symbol you write which step it represents. There are many other symbols, but it is advisable to stick to the most common ones, as you want your audience to understand the process you're describing. Too many specialized symbols just confuse them. So keep it simple and, if possible, stick to these basic shapes:

1. The long circle signifies the start or end of a process;

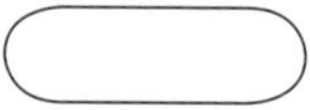

2. the rectangle shows instructions or actions; and

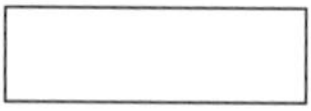

3. the diamond shows decisions that have to be taken.

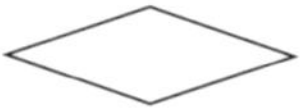

	True	False
1. Flowcharts show how a process fits together.	☐	☐
2. Diamonds can signify the start of a process.	☐	☐
3. Rectangles show instructions or actions.	☐	☐
4. Long circles symbolize decisions.	☐	☐
5. Only three symbols are used in flowcharts.	☐	☐

Lösungen

A. Bewerben

A1 List A: experience List B: salary List C: position

A2 job ad ▶ applica-tion ▶ shortlist
interview ▶ offer ▶ accept-ance

A3 1. present employer 2. application form 3. covering letter 4. educational background 5. marital status

A4 2. c 3. a 4. b 5. f 6. g 7. e

A5 2. a 3. c 4. d 5. f 6. b

A6 1. BE: holiday; AE: vacation
2. BE: programme; AE: program
3. BE: tick; AE: check
4. BE: fill in; AE: fill out

A7 2. permanent 3. senior
4. specialised 5. part-time
6. alphabetical

A8 4 2 6 3 5 1

A9 1. Mr 2. for your 3. would 4. to
5. the 6. you 7. my interview
8. I will 9. from Frankfurt on
10. I bring references

A10 2. I'd like to **discuss** (or: **talk about**) promotion prospects. 3. Could you **say** (or: **tell me**) something about the company management?
4. I **told you** (or: **said**) that I would contact you today. 5. I've had a lot of **experience** in this kind of work.
6. **Everything you've** (or: **Everything that you've**) told me has been most interesting. 7. For two years, I worked **at** Germelmann & Braun.
8. I would **appreciate hearing** from you as soon as possible.

A11 b i f h d a c g j e

A12 2. I enclose my CV and a copy of my school certificate. 3. I would like to arrange an appointment. 4. Is my application confidential? 5. I am available for interview at any time.
6. My last employer is willing to provide a reference. 7. My duties included commercial correspondence.

A13 2. interview 3. independent
4. ambitious 5. home page
6. probation period 7. contract
8. hopeful 9. resign 10. profession
11. enclosed

A14 2. g 3. b 4. f 5. a 6. c 7. h
8. e 9. j 10. i

A15 1. regional sales 2. foreign clients
3. the opportunity 4. flexible and willing 5. available for interview
6. references and testimonials

A16 2. Master of Business Administration
3. date of birth 4. overtime
5. sales representative 6. performance-related pay 7. Personal Assistant 8. Human Resources
9. Public Relations

B. Bei der Arbeit

B1 List A: repairs List B: equipment List C: scanner

B2 1. scissors 2. envelope 3. ballpoint
4. paper clip 5. desk 6. punch

B3 2. furniture 3. maintenance
4. security 5. shredder
6. calculator 7. printer

B4 2. a 6 3. e 10 4. b 9 5. c 8

B5 1. Ms Crawcour 2. for your 3. am

4. to seeing you in 5. will be 6. 3pm on 21st 7. you 8. that you can come at 9. you will find 10. to help you 11. call 12. you have 13. sincerely,

B6 2. Nice to meet you.
3. Glad you could come.
4. Did you have a good trip?
5. Please take a seat.
6. Make yourself at home.
7. Would you like a cup of coffee?

B7 a g b e c h d f

B8 1. 5 (The unnamed speaker who is making the introductions, Mr James, Herr Bremer, Frau Peters, Herr Weber)
2. 2 (Herr Bremer & Frau Peters)
3. 1 (Herr Weber)

B9 2. I suggest we meet in the lounge at 10. 3. I'll pick you up at the hotel at 11 o'clock. 4. May I invite you to meet me for lunch? 5. Let me know if you run into any difficulty. 6. Let's look at the main aspects we have to deal with here. 7. If you're ready, we can start straight away. 8. It's a pleasure to do business with you.

B10 2. opening session 3. keynote speaker 4. fact sheet 5. coffee break 6. conference timetable 7. name card

B11 *Your speech could be as follows:*
Good morning, ladies and gentlemen. Can you all hear me? My name's ... and I'd like to welcome you to the conference. I hope you all had a pleasant journey and that you find everything satisfactory.
Just a couple of points before we begin. First, if you need any help, please see me. I'll be at the main entrance. Next, do you all have a fact sheet? And a conference timetable and name card? Yes? Good. Next point: would you all please sign the attendance list? Thank you very much.
Right, we'll have a coffee break at 11o'clock and lunch will be served in the restaurant at 1pm.
Now, are there any questions?

B12 1. True 2. True 3. False 4. False 5. True

B13 1. to inform 2. discussing 3. mailing 4. to have 5. using 6. to deal

▶ Gebrauch von *remember, stop* und *go on*:

to remember + ing: sich erinnern, etwas getan zu haben
I ***remember checking*** *the cartridge some days ago.*

to remember to + Infinitiv: daran denken, etwas zu tun (= nicht vergessen, etwas zu tun)
Please ***remember to check*** *the cartridge once a week.*

to stop + ing: aufhören, etwas zu tun
We stopped working *on the accounts as we didn't have all of the documentation.*

to stop to + Infinitiv: aufhören, um etwas anderes zu tun
During the journey, ***I stopped to work*** *on my presentation.*

to go on (= continue) + ing: etwas weiterhin tun
I think we should ***go on discussing*** *this point till we've agreed.*

to go on to + Infinitiv: etwas (Neues) als Nächstes tun
Right, that point is settled – let's ***go on to discuss*** *the next one.*

B14 2. that is – d. h. 3. and the rest – usw. 4. compare – vgl. 5. for and on behalf of – i.A.

C. Die Firma

C1 List A: firm List B: section List C: medium-sized

C2 1. company 2. department 3. section 4. enterprise 5. firm 6. substantial

C3 1. d, e 2. c 3. a 4. b

C4 2. divide 3. sell 4. direct 5. execute 6. manage 7. equip 8. locate 9. promote

C5 a g b h c f d e

C6

C7 2. located 3. sections 4. in control 5. heads 6. responsibilities

C8 2. head 3. branch 4. boss 5. report 6. decide 7. retail 8. employee

C9 2. a 10 3. e 8 4. b 6 5. c 9

C10 1. financial director 2. industrial site 3. office premises 4. policy meeting 5. progress report 6. quality control 7. joint venture

C11 1. policy meeting 2. industrial site 3. office premises 4. financial director 5. progress report 6. quality control 7. joint venture

C12 2. First, I'll give you some **information** about the company structure.
3. Then I'll **explain to you** our hiring policy.
4. **Most of the producers** / **Most producers** in this field are based in Asia.
5. The management will be meeting on the first Tuesday of the month, **as usual**.
6. **The news is** good: sales increased 8% last month.

C13 2. The new company has a workforce of 28. 3. We've been investing in labour-saving technology. 4. We normally carry out repairs ourselves. 5. Herr Peterson is responsible for this part of the operation. 6. The technicians are responsible for monitoring safety. 7. All decisions about deliveries are made by Frau Berner. 8. We hand in a progress report to Frau Berner every month.

C14 1. False 2. True 3. False 4. True 5. True

C15 2. Chief Executive Officer 3. Chief Financial Officer 4. Company 5. Chamber of Commerce 6. Office of Fair Trading

D. Handel

D1 List A: invoice   List B: research   List C: shipment

D2 2. g   3. b   4. f   5. c   6. a   7. d

D3 1. favourable price   2. special price   3. competitive price   4. list price   5. bottom price   6. average price

D4 2. c 10   3. b 8   4. e 9   5. a 6

D5 2. estimate   3. plan   4. analyse   6. specialise   7. compete   8. average

D6 2. guarantee   3. delivery   4. forwarding   5. packaging/package   6. weight   7. sale   8. shipment   9. document / documentation   10. regulation   11. haulage   12. flight   13. storage   14. receipt / reception

D7 2. acceptable / accepted   3. analytical / analysed   4. guaranteed   5. informed / informative   6. profitable   7. strategic / strategical   8. structured / structural   9. transported / transportable

D8 2. list price   3. shipment   4. door-to-door   5. guarantee   6. special price   7. quotation

D9 2. don't you?   3. didn't we?   4. haven't you?   5. couldn't you?   6. isn't it?   7. shouldn't we?

> ▶ **Englische Frageanhängsel** (= *question tags*, z. B. *isn't it? couldn't we?*) dienen dazu, eine offene Position auszudrücken: *And your two-year service guarantee is included, isn't it?* Beachten Sie: *or?* ist **kein** englisches Frageanhängsel.

D10 2. delivery date   3. airtight packaging   4. air freight   5. forwarding agent   6. in transit   7. by sea

D11 1. check   2. checking   3. goods   4. bill   5. railway   6. railroad   7. post   8. mail   9. fund

D12 2. pricing   3. fee   4. bill   5. charge   6. expensive   7. goods   8. sell

D13 Susanne Briegel called from Essen. She says that Leyland Shipping phoned her and said that they will deliver Order No. 133 (gross weight 5.2 t) tomorrow. It's not necessary to call her back.

D14 2. We can offer you door-to-door delivery.   3. Deliveries have to be brought forward by two months.   4. Our customers want to know the price of the product.   5. We'll sell below market price to get rid of the stock.   6. We've been able to estimate the likely costs.   7. Could you give me a guarantee on that?   8. $770 for 10 units – that's an average price of $77.   9. We'll need to make another $450 to break even.   10. There's a delivery charge for each order.

D15 1. strong   2. roughly   3. operate   4. advertising   5. network   6. discount

D16 2. unique selling point   3. Personal Identification Number   4. business to business   5. business to customer   6. just in time   7. for the attention of   8. International Money Order   9. do-it-yourself store   10. computer-aided design   11. desktop publishing   12. information technology

E. Geschäftsreisen

E1 List A: problem areas List B: single room List C: publicity video

E2 1. pick me up 2. due to 3. by 1430hr 4. publicity video 5. key issues.

E3 d h c e a f b g

E4 2. security check 3. carry-on bag 4. car hire 5. domestic flight 6. intermediate stop 7. shuttle service 8. local time 9. return ticket

E5 2. proposed – proposal 3. agreed – agreement 4. approved – approval 5. solved – solution 6. decisive / deciding – decision 7. advised / advisory – advice

E6 2. b 3. e 4. c 5. f 6. d 7. a

E7 1. order 2. suggest 3. insist 4. agree 5. meet

E8 2. convey an idea 3. raise (any) questions 4. glitch 5. highlight 6. screen 7. comparison

E9 1. U-Bahn 2. lift 3. second floor 4. third floor

E10 1. till 2. by 3. by 4. till

E11 1. My 2. I have an 3. to meet 4. Mrs 5. And we 6. on 7. I'm 8. I'm 9. to 10. Mrs 11. a cup of 12. would be

E12 1. Do you enjoy the travel side of your work, Mr Jackson? 2. Do you travel a lot? 3. And it's a break from the daily grind, isn't it? 4. I know the feeling! 5. OK, we'll try and go easy on you! 6. How do you mean?

E13 2. How will I recognise you?
3. Has there been a message for me, please? 4. I hope you find everything to your satisfaction.
5. Should you need any help, please let me know. 6. Don't hesitate to raise questions at any time.
7. Are there any further questions?
8. I'd like to show you a short video.
9. Could you tell me the price, please?
10. Would this arrangement be convenient for you? 11. On the face of it, the idea looks good. 12. Could you keep the offer open for another two weeks? 13. We'd have to insist on an advance payment.

E14 2. automated teller machine *(= Geldautomat)* 3. compact disc 4. overhead projector 5. video conference 6. video cassette recorder 7. visual display unit

Dt.: bis

Engl.: till (= *die ganze Zeit über bis*)	Engl.: by (= *nicht später als*)
<u>*Beispiele:*</u>	
Wir dürfen das Geld bis Ende Februar behalten.	We can keep the money **till** the end of February.
Der Vertrag muss bis Freitag verhandelt werden.	The contract must be negotiated **by** Friday.
You can reach us **till** Monday morning by phone.	I'll call you **by** 9.30.

F. Handelskorrespondenz und Telefonieren

F1 List A: order List B: cell phone List C: hang up

F2

enquiry ▶ offer ▶ payment

order ▶ confirmation ▶ delivery

F3 2. c 3. a 4. f 5. e 6. b

F4 2. c/d 3. b 4. c/d 5. a 6. e

F5 1. meeting 2. leaflet 3. specific 4. suits 5.early

F6 b a d c e

F7 1. This is Peter Reinhardt. I'm calling from Hamburg and would like to speak to Ms Johnson, please.
2. I'm afraid she's on the other line at the moment, Herr Reinhardt. Perhaps I can help you?
3. Yes, please tell Ms Johnson that we'll order the 'de Luxe' model.
4. The 'de Luxe' model.
5. But only if you can deliver this month. Would you run that back to me, please?
6. OK. You'll order the 'de Luxe' model if we can deliver this month.
7. Right.
8. Very well, Herr Reinhardt. I'll pass that on. You'll be hearing from Ms Johnson very soon. Thank you for calling.

F8 2. a 3. e 4. c 5. d 6. g 7. b

F9 2. We would **appreciate receiving** your reply soon. 3. **Despite** the damage (or: **In spite of** the damage), the goods are still useable.
4. The orders section has **its own website** (or: **a website of its own**). 5. **At the moment**, Frau Bach isn't in. Can she call you back? 6. Could you use different packaging, **without charging extra**?

F11 1. True 2. False 3. True 4. False 5. False 6. False 7. True

F12 1. neighbor 2. theatre 3. modeled 4. defence 5. dialog 6. anaesthetic

▶ Beispiele unterschiedlicher Schreibweisen:
<u>Spelling differences</u>

British English: **our** / American English: **or**
BE: favourite / AE: favorite
BE: labour / AE: labor

British English: **re** / American English: **er**
BE: centre / AE: center
BE: kilometre / AE: kilometer

British English: **ll** / American English: **l**
BE: cancelled / AE: canceled
BE: travelled / AE: traveled

British English: **c** / American English: **s**
BE: licence / AE: license
BE: offence / AE: offense

British English: **logue** / American English: **log**
BE: catalogue / AE: catalog
BE: monologue / AE: monolog

British English: **ae** / American English: **e**
BE: orthopaedic / AE: orthopedic
BE: archaeology / AE: archeology

F13 2. ... I'll have to cancel the order. 3. Are you calling about the catalogues? 4. May I speak to the person responsible for sales? 5. Could I speak to someone about your delivery charges? 6. Call me back to confirm that, would you, please? (Or: Would you call me back to confirm that, please?) 7. I'll phone you again as soon as possible. 8. Would you run that through again, please? 9. The country code for Germany is 49. 10. Do call me again if I can be of any help.

F14 2. all the best 3. Attention 4. by the way 5. for your information 6. hope this helps 7. in my opinion 8. in other words 9. talk to you later

G. Kommunikative Strategien

G1 List A: repair List B: loss
List C: error

G2 2. reimburse / reimbursement
3. disappoint/ disappointment
4. delay / delay
5. damage / damage
6. disappear / disappearance
7. annoy / annoyance

G3 2. considerable difficulties
3. immediately 4. urgently
5. in the circumstances
6. compensation
7. delay

G4 b f c a e d

G5 2. discount 3. mistake 4. repair 5. explanation 6. solution 7. dispute

G6 2. b 3. f 4. d 5. a 6. e

G7 Baldry: 1 Daniels: 2 Rutter: 3

G8 2. b 3. f 4. e 5. c 6. a

G9 2. d + f 3. a + k 4. g + h 5. i + j 6. b + l

G10 2. a 3. b 4. d 5. f 6. e

G11 1. d 2. c 3. a 4. e 5. b

G12 2. The terms of the contract are quite clear. 3. We wish to express our great regret. 4. Please accept our apologies. 5. Perhaps I could pick up on that point. 6. May I ask a question here? 7. Could I just come in here? 8. Let me complete my point, please.

G13 1. False 2. True 3. False 4. True 5. True

G14 3. tomorrow 4. for 5. accommodation 6. additional 7. as soon as possible 8. be 9. before 10. see 11. could 12. committee 13. see you 14. especially 15. face to face 16. including 17. information 18. message 19. Oh, I see 20. please 21. possible 22. are 23. received 24. Regards 25. speaker 26. thanks 27. you 28. would 29. your 30. Yours

H. Marketing & Werbung

H1 List A: budget List B: client
List C: slogan

H2 2. i 15 3. g 16 4. h 20 5. a 18 6. e 19 7. b 14 8. j 12 9. c 17 10. d 11

H3 Company's letter: 4, 5, 6, 7, 10
Market research report: 2, 3, 8, 9

H4 2. prospects 3. specifications 4. rivals 5. user-friendly 6. catalogue

H5 1. True 2. True 3. False 4. True 5. False 6. True

H6 ~~programms~~ → programmes (or: programs)
~~developement~~ → development
~~catagories~~ → categories
~~arguement~~ → argument
~~commitee~~ → committee
~~seperately~~ → separately

H7 2. public opinion 3. random sample 4. income group 5. sole earner 6. consumer behaviour 7. spending habits 8. domestic consumption

H8 2. word-of-mouth advertising 3. sales campaign 4. purchasing power 5. trade fair 6. business card 7. poster 8. price list 9. feedback

H9 2. The Danish market is apparently larger than expected. 3. We have a good 15% share of the market. 4. 40% of the population are in the middle-income group. 5. We definitely want to know the size of the market. 6. Have you had any feedback about the advert yet? 7. We're dealing with an entirely new territory. 8. That's the main advantage of this particular model. 9. Advertising takes up 15% of our total budget. 10. What target group are you aiming at? 11. This product will sell itself. 12. Could you explain the thinking behind the campaign?

H10 Dear Editor,
We are a new company in your area and begin production on 12 July. We feel sure that your readers will be interested in this development. Please feel free to publish all or part of the attached information and pictures. You will find more details on our website: www.okpick.com
If you would like to arrange an interview or photo-session, we would be very happy to hear from you. In the meantime, I am sending, in the attachments, a short text on our company, plus photos which I hope you will use in your report.
Yours faithfully,

H11 a g b e d h c f

H12 2. headquarters 3. cost-benefit analysis 4. Gross National Product 5. Gross Domestic Product 6. per annum 7. in charge 8. Corporation

H13 Strengths Weaknesses Opportunities Threats

I. Internationaler Handel

I1 List A: European Union
List B: insurance certificate
List C: economic growth

I2 1. g 10 3. a 14 4. b 9 5. e 12 6. d 8 7. c 13

I3 1. Bulgarian 2. (the) Czech Republic 3. Denmark 4. Estonia 5. Finnish 6. German 7. Greece 8. Irish 9. Italy 10. Latvia 11. Maltese 12. Dutch 13. Polish 14. Portugal 15. Romania 16. Slovakian 17. Spain 18. British

I4 A.
2. negotiate 3. know-how 4. equipment 5. Letter of Intent 6. losses 7. own

B.
b c a d e

I5 1. declare 2. consider 3. form 4. co-operate 5. attach 6. accept 7. continue 8. agree 9. approve

I6 2. probable 3. probable 4. probable 5. improbable 6. certain 7. probable 8. only possible 9. certain

I7 2. wealth 3. poverty 4. development 5. sustainable 6. global 7. environment 8. wastage

I8 2. We are now discovering **what** is meant by globalisation. 3. The representatives have no **knowledge** of German. 4. **Your two orders** (or: **Both (of) your orders**) have been despatched by air freight. 5. Welcome **to** Germany! 6. Our first priority is **to save money**, then we'll think about importing.

I9 2. living standard 3. poverty line 4. economic growth 5. development aid 6. energy policy 7. greenhouse effect 8. ozone hole 9. noise pollution 10. waste disposal 11. GM food 12. fossil fuels 13. carbon dioxide

I10 h d a f b i c k g e

I11 1. mail 2. newsagent 3. petrol 4. general 5. fall 6. inventory

I12 1. customs invoice 2. insurance policy 3. health certificate 4. import permit 5. delivery order

I13 2. We don't expect that the market will pick up again before December. 3. The decline has been sharper this year. 4. How can we decide what certificates are needed? 5. Exports fell by €1000 to €12000. 6. Right now, the market is weakening. 7. Which currency would we have to pay in?

I14 2. Central European Time 3. Eastern European Time 4. International Monetary Fund 5. World Trade Organisation 6. New York Stock Exchange 7. European Central Bank 8. International Chamber of Commerce 9. Single Administrative Document

I15

EXW	**EX W**orks	*ab Werk*
FCA	**F**ree **c**arrier	*frei Frachtführer*
FAS	**F**ree **A**longside **S**hip	*frei längsseits Schiff*
FOB	**F**ree **O**n **B**oard	*frei an Bord*
CFR	**C**ost And **Fr**eight	*Kosten und Fracht (nur für Schiffstransporte)*
CIF	**C**ost **I**nsurance **F**reight	*Kosten, Versicherung und Fracht bis zum Bestimmungshafen/Bestimmungsort*
CPT	**C**arriage **P**aid **T**o	*Fracht, Porto bezahlt bis*
CIP	**C**arriage **I**nsurance **P**aid	*Fracht, Porto und Versicherung bezahlt bis*
DAF	**D**elivered **A**t **F**rontier	*frei Grenze*
DES	**D**elivered **E**x **S**hip	*frei ab Schiff*
DEQ	**D**elivered **E**x **Q**uay	*frei ab Kai*
DDU	**D**elivery **D**uty **U**npaid	*frei unverzollt*
DDP	**D**elivery **D**uty **P**aid	*frei verzollt*

J. Mengenangaben

J1 List A: fraction List B: deduct
List C: measured

J2 2. percentage 3. calculate
4. convert 5. fraction 6. subtract

J3 A.
2. Monday 3. Tuesday 4. Wednesday 5. Thursday 6. Friday
7. Saturday

B.
1. January 2. February 3. March
4. April 5. May 6. June 7. July
8. August 9. September 10. October 11. November 12. December

J4 We pay ...: 3, 4, 7, 11, 12, 13
We pay for ...: 2, 5, 6, 8, 9, 10, 14

J5 2. 12th 3. 1st 4. 17th 5. 23rd
6. 25th 7. 25th 8. 18th 9. 29th
10. 29th 11. 16th 12. 19th

J6 A.
15 9 4 36

B.
2. a 3. d 4. c 5. e

J7 a f b h c e d g

J8 B.
1. of three 2. 5th of September
3. past ten 4. 11th of February

C.

	BE	AE
the twenty-second of May	22/05	05/22
the first of October	01/10	10/01
the tenth of January	10/01	01/10
the eighth of September	08/09	09/08

J9 2. 50th 3. a / per 4. a 5. an
6. of an 7. second-biggest
8. third-best 9. double-digit / double-figure 10. ratio 11. even / odd 12. numerical 13. a 14. twice
15. up

J10 2. at half past eight 3. at all times
4. ten thousand dollars 5. 5.5% x £2,000 6. every third customer
7. three times as many 8. twice as much

J11 1. 1.40 2. 1.59 3. 0.19

J12 2. Each month, you will receive a statement. 3. These charges are adjusted from time to time. 4. We will inform you about this in advance. 5. Are there any charges other than interest? 6. They normally pay within 30 days. 7. They earn about 5% above the national average.

J13 2. 6% x £1800
3. 14.3% x €3,500
4. 250 @ €6.20 (or: 250 x €6.20)
5. 2/3 x €300
6. 0.5%

J14 2. estimated time of arrival
3. between 12 midnight & 12 noon
4. between 12 noon & 12 midnight

K. Diagramme & Statistik

K1 2. a 3. e 4. d 5. c

K2 1. True 2. True 3. False 4. True
5. False 6. True 7. True 8. True
9. True

K3 1. half as many again 2. have doubled 3. have tripled 4. three times as many units 5. third-smallest 6. little increase

7. an average of one a month

K4 3 5 1 2 4

K5 2. Austria, Greece
3. Denmark, Italy, Greece
4. Italy, Malta 5. Germany
6. two 7. three 8. four

K6 1. park and ride 2. Research & Development 3. bed and breakfast 4. postage and packing 5. fire and theft 6. profit and loss

K7 1. pie chart 2. mean value
3. variation 4. distribution
5. flowchart 6. prospects
7. annually

K8 1. True 2. True 3. False 4. True
5. False 6. False

K9 2. highlight 3. fluctuation
4. outline 5. flow 6. increase
7. decline 8. expectation / expectancy 9. peak

K10 2. Well, we expect a fall-off at the end of the summer, don't we?
3. But this is worrying. Look – the decline is much stronger than this time last year. 4. The general recession is still hurting the trade, of course. So sales will probably remain flat till November. 5. Then they're likely to pick up over the Christmas period? 6. Yes. 7. And again in the spring? 8. Yes. Actually, prospects are pretty good for next year. Have you looked at the advance orders we've received?

K11 1. True 2. False 3. True 4. False
5. False